Adapting to Change

Adapting to Change

The Business of Climate Resilience

Ann Goodman

Adapting to Change: The Business of Climate Resilience
Copyright © Business Expert Press, LLC, 2016.

First published in 2016 by
Business Expert Press, LLC
222 East 46th Street, New York, NY 10017
www.businessexpertpress.com

ISBN-13: 978-1-63157-144-2 (paperback)
ISBN-13: 978-1-63157-145-9 (e-book)

Business Expert Press Giving Voice to Values on Business Ethics
and Corporate Social Responsibility Collection

Collection ISSN: 2333-8806 (print)
Collection ISSN: 2333-8814 (electronic)

Cover and interior design by S4Carlisle Publishing Services
Private Ltd., Chennai, India

First edition: 2016

10 9 8 7 6 5 4 3 2 1

Printed in the United States of America.

In memory of Cynthia Philip, who inspired by example and encouraged through word and deed

Abstract

This book examines emerging business reactions to, plans, and preparations for climate events (e.g., fires, storms, floods, and hurricanes) and trends (e.g., droughts) from leading companies in strategic sectors: technology, telecommunications, food, banking, and insurance.

Each profile, from which each chapter in the table of contents, above, is derived, illustrates one of five themes:

  i. Responding to weather;
 ii. Learning from disaster;
iii. Doing more with less;
 iv. Taking a risk—and managing it;
  v. communicating change, collaborating on climate

Informed by the 2015 COP 21 climate meetings in Paris, the book pays special attention to evolving communications strategies that encourage resilience, both inside the company—with managers and employees—and externally—supply and value chain, community, investors, others—to moderate business and human risk. The book also looks at the private–public sector interaction in this area, how it has or hasn't worked well, what each might best offer the other, along with emerging responses.

Chapters stress evolving solutions to real problems that real companies are facing in real time. It is best read as a snapshot in time, with the understanding that companies' resilience plans are evolving, along with their practical and pragmatic approaches in response to our changing climate—and, critically, to their changing business goals.

Significantly, the book focuses on business opportunities innovative company leaders—with substantial input from employees, among other stakeholders—are already exploring in response to the changing climate.

The target audience includes business students and practitioners, including business communications professionals; it also includes any lay person interested in this or a related topic.

Readers will benefit from learning about how real companies with real problems are facing a real-time crisis that affects all of us—and how they're using business acumen to create solutions to a fast-changing situation predicated on uncertainty.

The author, Ann Goodman, PhD, is a sustainability professional with 25 years of experience in the field as a professor, journalist, for- and non-profit executive. Her initial interest in sustainability was sparked by her concern about the changing climate and how business might help solve the problem. After broadening her sustainability knowledge and activities, she has returned to this initial climate concern, in part inspired by the increase in climate disasters—three of which she has lived through.

Keywords

business; Climate change/adaptation; disaster; global warming; green; sustainability; resilience; risk; risk management; sustainable development; uncertainty; weather; UN; IPCC; NCA; COP 21

Contents

Preface

Climate, Disaster, Resilience, Hope

Does climate change doom us? The science and numbers are stacked against us. We've known for a century that the climate is warming and that the rise in temperatures is speeding up because we're emitting greenhouse gases (GHGs).[1]

We're on our way to an increase of 4° Celsius by 2050 unless we significantly curb emissions—starting now.[2] If we don't, we'll see even greater sea level rise,[3] frightening climate-related weather events,[4] mounting health problems,[5] and more deaths.[6]

This is no longer abstraction: I've lived through three climate-related crises, including Hurricanes Sandy in New York City and Irene in upstate New York in autumn 2012, as well as the freak ice storm during the equivalent of summer in northern Thailand in early 2013.

These experiences aren't fun—though Sandy happened around Halloween, and, thanks to a small backup generator in my apartment building in lower Manhattan (where there was no power or water), some neighbors got together in the lobby to drink wine and watch a scary film or two.

We had it relatively easy; all we had to do was walk a mile (albeit with no street lights at night) to charge our cell phones and buy bottled water

---

[1]Sobel, Adam. (2014). *Storm Surge: Hurricane Sandy, Our Changing Climate, and Extreme Weather of the Past and Future.* New York, NY: HarperCollins.

[2]International Energy Agency. (2015) "Publications: Scenarios and Projections." Accessed August 17, 2015. http://www.iea.org/publications/scenariosandprojections/

[3]Sobel, Adam. (2014). *Storm Surge: Hurricane Sandy, Our Changing Climate, and Extreme Weather of the Past and Future.* New York, NY: HarperCollins.

[4]Ibid.

[5]National Climate Assessment 2014. 221–256; Lancet report 2015.

[6]Vidal, John. (2009). "Global Warming Causes 300,000 Deaths a Year, Says Kofi Annan Thinktank." *The Guardian,* May 29, 2009, accessed November 19, 2015. http://www.theguardian.com/environment/2009/may/29/1.

at the 7–Eleven. In other parts of the city, there were massive floods, toppled buildings, injured people, and more.

Yet, despite the shattering statistics and personal experiences, my human nature doesn't let me contemplate doom as the ultimate outcome of what most certainly is one of the greatest crises of our time, if not all time (otherwise, I wouldn't have spent the last quarter century working on this issue, nor would I have spent two years putting together this book).

That's not to say that there's an easy fix. If that were the case, we'd have fixed it by now.

Nor do I believe that business—the subject of this book—can fix it all, or that it is the cause of all that's wrong. What's wrong is much more complex, involving patterns of human psychology and interaction that underlie political and other power struggles, some of which, of course, play out in business and between the public and private sectors.

What has lifted my spirits while researching, reporting, and writing this book are my countless encounters with the apparently endlessly creative, enthusiastic human spirit. Whether talking with business people or academics or lay folk, what is inspiring is the common will to do something— a number of things, actually—to help us escape the trap of climate doom.

Yes, I'm inspired by human ingenuity. And I'm finding it throughout the business world. No, not in every company, to be sure (though there may be rising will to do something, think and act differently, even among those companies that have resisted for too long).

What I've found is that the changing climate can inspire positive business change. Indeed, changing needs probably always have inspired changing practices, engendering business solutions along the way. Business is good at responding to new needs. And if ever there was a need to respond, it's now.

Why are those companies that are acting to prevent climate disaster (even as we seem to face multiple climate-related threats more and more frequently) doing so? Partly, it's self-preservation. "Do nothing" is always a possibility, and that's what, collectively, we've been doing for so long that today we're facing climate-related risks regularly. But is that how we're constructed—to do nothing? Don't we move and change in the face of threats, at least those of us who survive?

Partly, too, in the case of business, acting on the imminent climate threat may avert financial—and potentially much greater—loss, or even garner a profit. Though, to be sure, those companies acting on the threat are doing so partly because it's the right thing to do—for the business, customers, employees, investors, communities, the planet, civilization, and fellow human beings. Business, after all, is made up of people, and we all have, somewhere inside, an empathetic bone.

I'm not an apologist for business. But there are some misunderstandings about business, especially in connection with climate change.

For one thing, there's no one common face of business, as when we talk of the private *versus* public sectors. Yes, business is a sector, as are government and civil society—all three of which have contributed to the climate predicament, if unwittingly, and all three of which must work together to resolve it, perhaps in public–private partnerships, or PPPs.

Business is a sector, but it's made up of individual companies, in turn made up of individual people. It's not a monolithic construct. As in other parts of life and society, there are leaders and laggards, good guys and bad guys.

In this book, my aim is to spotlight activities of some (though certainly not all) of the good guys: leaders, who, in the face of what they agree is a changing climate—which often they have experienced first- or second-hand—are changing the way they do business, including the what and how and sometimes where.

These leaders aren't just reacting to a potentially bad business climate (though if the climate gets bad enough, there won't be much business to be done). Often companies, like people, really want to do something good—and are looking to accomplish this as best they can, as soon as possible, sometimes in the face of obstacles.

Nor do I mean to suggest that the companies profiled in this book are perfect. No company is perfect, and neither are many people. Certainly, when it comes to climate change, there's hardly a company without a carbon footprint, somewhere along the supply and value chain.

Instead, what I hope to show here is that, increasingly, in the face of the changes we see every day in all parts of the world, some of the more courageous companies are indeed taking steps—sometimes big, but often small and simple, steps with far-reaching ramifications—to achieve climate resilience.

That means, first of all, accepting climate change as a scientific (and common-sense) fact. It also usually means trying to temper—even eliminate, if, perhaps over the long term—the chief cause, GHGs emitted by burning fossil fuels. It means preparing—in many ways—for what we know will be increasingly frequent, intense, and urgent weather events. Perhaps most important, it means preparing for the unknown (along with the known).

Yes, some of this is an outgrowth of business as usual: taking steps to ensure business continuity, to strengthen the supply chain, to manage and, as far as possible, reduce risk—of all sorts—for the company and its stakeholders.

More importantly: A lot of climate resilience is about creativity—about hope and life and the future. And that's the inspiring part, the part that helps to restore faith (at least mine) in the human species.

Acknowledgments

Many individuals and organizations contributed their time and insight to this book.

Special thanks go to my editor, Mary Gentile and to my publishers at BEP.

Much gratitude to the many people at the companies profiled here, who shared their experiences in many interviews.

Additional thanks go to a number of colleagues, who offered special insight, including my principal researcher, Megan Helseth, Chris Walker of WBCSD, Brendan LeBlanc, Dan Kreeger of ACCO, Joyce Coffee of ND GAIN, Debbra Johnson, Emilie Mazzacurati, Jean Rogers of SASB, Dawn Rittenhouse of DuPont, Bernhard Frey of the UN Global Compact, Jeff Peck, Cynthia Thompson and Prakash Sethi of CUNY's Zicklin School of Business, Elke Weber of Columbia Business School, among many others, too numerous to list here. My gratitude goes also to editors at Greenbiz.com, who published early versions of several chapters. And, of course, I thank my many friends around the globe who offered invaluable support in manifold ways.

Finally, this undertaking would not have been possible without all those who find hope in the face of change and inspire others through positive innovation.

Introduction

Business in a Changing World: Climate, Economy, Technology—And Doing More, Faster, With Less

It's not news that the world is changing. It's always done so. But some changes seem a lot bigger and faster today than they did in the past—at least than they did in the second half of the 20th century.

Today we're living with several monumental, ongoing changes, among them: a global economy so uncertain, that, on a given day, multiple stories in the same newspaper suggest contradictory paths it might take; a global society so tied to fast-paced technology, that we can get virtually simultaneous photos, videos, text messages and social media accounts of a single happening anywhere in the world almost instantly; a world so bent on moving forward faster, that as soon as we master one technology, we're already on the next; and a world where natural resources are depleted and we must find innovative solutions for everything we need and want to do with less.[7]

As if all this weren't enough, big changes are happening in our climate. Climate change isn't new. The climate has been changing because of human activity since the Industrial Revolution, when we began sending large amounts of greenhouse gas (GHGs) emissions into the atmosphere.[8] We've known for a century that the climate is warming, and that the increase in average global temperature is speeding up because we continue to emit greenhouse gases.[9] In 2013, the National Oceanic and Atmospheric

---

[7]My friend Andrew Winston has described some of this—and more—in his 2014 book *The Big Pivot: Radically Practical Strategies for a Hotter, Scarcer, and More Open World.*

[8]NASA: In its Fourth Assessment Report, the IPCC concluded there's a more than 90 percent probability that human activities over the past 250 years have warmed our planet.

[9]Sobel, Adam. (2014). *Storm Surge: Hurricane Sandy, Our Changing Climate, and Extreme Weather of the Past and Future.* New York, NY: HarperCollins.

Administration (NOAA) reported that carbon dioxide levels had surpassed 400 parts per million, the highest in millions of years.[10]

It's also not news that business, empowered by the Industrial Revolution, has long contributed vast quantities of GHGs to the atmosphere. A 2013 study found that just 90 companies have emitted almost two-thirds of GHG emissions generated since the beginning of the Industrial Revolution.[11] Yet, by the same token, many companies have long been concerned about the environment and have worked to improve it—or at the very least not to harm it further.

Some companies have been worried about the effects of mounting GHG emissions for decades, and they've been taking steps to reduce their output. Some have done so because their stakeholders (customers, shareholders, employees, among others) care. Some do it because it's good for business; it can reduce costs, for instance, or even enhance revenue. Some do it because it's the right thing. And some do it for all those reasons, and more.

Nonetheless, while we've known about negative effects of GHGs on the climate for a long time, until recently, what's escaped so many of us—business included—is that dangers of those effects are already upon us.[12] With the advent of highly unusual, frightening weather events[13]—in the United States perhaps epitomized by Hurricane Sandy in 2012—it's been

---

[10]NASA. (2015). "Greenhouse Gas Benchmark Reached." Accessed January 4, 2016. http://research.noaa.gov/News/NewsArchive/LatestNews/TabId/684/ArtMID/1768/ArticleID/11153/Greenhouse-gas-benchmark-reached-.aspx.

[11]Heede, Richard. "Tracing Anthropogenic Carbon Dioxide And Methane Emissions To Fossil Fuel And Cement Producers, 1854–2010". *Climatic Change* 122.1–2 (2013): 229–241.

[12]It is impossible to be absolutely certain about all the disaster-related effects of climate change, owing to the intrinsic uncertainty in the climate projections, the diverse and rapidly changing nature of community vulnerability, and the random nature of individual extreme events. However, there is plenty of information on the serious impacts of events that have occurred in past decades, and on this basis alone there is much to be concerned about. "Direct Observations Of Recent Climate Change - Summary For Policymakers". Ipcc.ch. N.p., 2016. Web. 12 July 2016.

[13] Weather is the set of meteorological conditions—wind, rain, snow, sunshine, temperature, etc.—at a particular time and place. By contrast, the term "climate" describes the overall long-term characteristics of the weather experienced at a place. The climate therefore can be thought of as a long-term summary of weather conditions, taking account of the *average*

hard to ignore our changing climate (in spite of some special interests that would have us doubt our senses).[14]

Business hasn't been immune to this changing reality. Nor has it been unconcerned or unaware. Too many US-based companies, small and large, were directly hurt by Sandy, and Hurricane Katrina 7 years earlier. Many saw facilities, supply chains, employees, or customers affected by the Sendai earthquake and tsunami in Japan 2011, the floods in Thailand 2011, and Typhoon Haiyan in the Philippines 2013. And those are just a sampling of the one-off shocks.[15] Business is also affected by ongoing problematic weather trends, like drought in the western US.[16]

In the face of mounting signs of climate change and its effects, business awareness is growing rapidly. Many companies are concerned, and some are trying to adapt in a variety of ways. This adaptive business response is still in its early stages, though the trend made major strides during Conference of the Parties (COP) 21 in Paris in December 2015, where companies made significant commitments to reduce GHGs. Indeed, a spring 2015 corporate adaptation survey found that while a majority of responding companies are monitoring climate change risk, and half are in the process of developing (or anticipate creating) adaptation plans or other

---

conditions as well as the *variability of these* conditions. "Direct Observations Of Recent Climate Change - Summary For Policymakers". Ipcc.ch. N.p., 2016. Web. 12 July 2016.

[14]Oreskes, Naomi. (2010). *Merchants of Doubt: How a Handful Scientists Obscured the Truth on Issues from Tobacco Smoke to Global Warming.* London: Bloomsbury Press.

[15]The frequency of heavy precipitation events has increased over most land areas, which is consistent with global warming and the observed increases of atmospheric water vapor. The higher the temperature of the air, the greater the amount of water vapor it can hold (the increase being about 7% for each 1°C increase in temperature) and hence the greater amount of moisture available for precipitation. "Direct Observations Of Recent Climate Change - Summary For Policymakers". Ipcc.ch. N.p., 2016. Web. 12 July 2016.

[16] More intense and longer droughts have been observed over wider areas since the 1970s, particularly in the tropics and subtropics. Higher temperatures and decreased precipitation have increased the prevalence of drier conditions as well as contributing to changes in the distribution of droughts. Changes in sea surface temperatures, wind patterns, and decreased snow pack and snow cover also have been linked to changing drought occurrence. "Direct Observations Of Recent Climate Change - Summary For Policymakers". Ipcc.ch. N.p., 2016. Web. 12 July 2016.

preparations to deal with climate change risk, almost 30 percent have no plan in place.[17] What's more, what's meant by "adaptation" or related terms like "resilience" varies widely from one company to another.

Emerging business approaches to climate resilience—simply put, the will and action to withstand, to continue, to protect, to prepare and, perhaps most important, to change—are on stage in the pages to come. The leaders profiled here are grappling with climate change today, before it becomes an emergency.[18] Even as they continue to develop new ways to handle the changing climate, they share what they're already doing.[19]

As extreme weather events and trends proliferate worldwide, it's becoming clearer that we're already living in a changing climate. And with extremes come the recognition that preparedness is essential to avoid the emergency of disaster—and, eventually, that preventing the worst

---

[17]From consulting firm Four Twenty-Seven and the University of Notre Dame Global Adaptation Index (ND-GAIN). Seville, Aleka, and Colin Gannon. (2015). "2015 Corporate Adaptation Survey." BSR, May 2015. p. 17. http://gain.org/sites/default/files/2015%20Corporate%20Adaptation%20Survey.pdf.

[18]Natural hazards by themselves do not cause disasters–it is the combination of an exposed, vulnerable and ill prepared population or community with a hazard event that results in a disaster. Climate change will therefore affect disaster risks in two ways, firstly through the likely increase in weather and climate hazards, and secondly through increases in the vulnerability of communities to natural hazards, particularly through ecosystem degradation, reductions in water and food availability, and changes to livelihoods. Climate change will add yet another stress to those of environmental degradation and rapid unplanned urban growth, further reducing communities' abilities to cope with even the existing levels of weather hazards. United Nations International Strategy for Disaster Reduction,. Climate Change And Disaster Risk Reduction. Geneva: N.p., 2008. Web. 10 July 2016. Briefing Note 1.

[19]IPCC definitions of resilience and adaptation:

Adaptation: The process of adjustment to actual or expected climate and its effects. In human systems, adaptation seeks to moderate harm or exploit beneficial opportunities. In natural systems, human intervention may facilitate adjustment to expected climate and its effects.

Resilience: The capacity of a social–ecological system to cope with a hazardous event or disturbance, responding or reorganizing in ways that maintain its essential function, identity, and structure, while also maintaining the capacity for adaptation, learning, and transformation. Direct Observations Of Recent Climate Change—Summary For Policymakers". Ipcc.ch. N.p., 2016. Web. 12 July 2016.

by adapting to the changing climate is essential. As awareness of climate risks and our need to adapt has grown in the past several years, there has been greater tendency in both public and private sectors to link the two, in efforts to improve both.

A key example is the UNISDR (United Nations International Strategy for Disaster Reduction) ARISE (Private Sector Alliance for Risk Sensitive Investment), supported by governments, business, NGOs and others, which addresses natural and man-made disasters, as well as sudden and creeping events often linked to climate change, including drought and sea-level rise. Unsurprisingly, the value of programs like ARISE and related efforts that connect climate, disasters and resilience or adaptation, are often recognized initially by those schooled in sustainability, whether in the public or private sectors, long before those in other sectors.

The main reason: Over the past several decades, sustainability practitioners and the sustainability function across sectors has housed all things environmental, including climate. And, while many are beginning to realize that climate change is more than an environmental issue, in professional circles, climate change, for the time being, remains largely the bailiwick of the sustainability office.[20]

As climate presents increasing risks, some companies are beginning to merge risk and sustainability to better understand potential risks to the entire enterprise (Enterprise Risk Management). Indeed, other risks, such as social or political risks, which can be equally disruptive to the business, are often linked to climate risk, as in the Pentagon's 2014 report *Climate Change Adaptation Roadmap*.[21] So, for instance, food shortages, sometimes brought about by changing climate conditions, can lead to social and political unrest or worse (e.g., Arab Spring and the conflict

---

[20]Among others, the Pope has emphasized that climate is among a number of moral issues to reckon with; *Risky Business: The Economic Risks of Climate Change in the United States*, endorsed by respected economic luminaries, including two former Secretaries of the Treasury from both parties, has pointed out economic relevance; and Dale Jamieson's 2014 book Reason in a Dark Time has linked economics and morality.

[21]The Department of Defense. (2015). "2014 Climate Change Adaptation Roadmap." Accessed November 19, 2015. http://www.acq.osd.mil/ie/download/CCARprint_wForeword_c.pdf.

in Syria[22]). In the World Economic Forum's (WEF) top five global risks of 2014, climate change ranked fourth in terms of likelihood and second in terms of impact; while in the WEF Global Risks Report released in January 2016, it had leaped to the number one slot in terms of risk impact.

Nonetheless, as awareness of multiple risks and multiple links grows, what's heartening is how, in the face of potentially frightening change, companies also change. In fact, it's inspiring to see some of what's best in the human species—ingenuity, creativity, innovation—brought to life in companies that, when faced with a changing reality, are forging new business paths and pursuing new opportunities.

In some ways, this is nothing new. Like people, business, faced with change, often changes nimbly. Also like people, business is often very creative when faced with new circumstances. And, like people, business often finds new ways of working, given new realities.

All this is not to say that all business is perfect, as it responds to climate change and makes changes to adapt to it, even as it tries to stem the emissions that are worsening it. Nor would it be correct to suggest that there isn't more that business can and should do—even leading companies.

The large companies profiled here are all publicly traded. They're well-known brand names. For the most part, they're multinationals. They report to shareholders and are scrutinized by government. So in some ways, they have more incentive—obligation, in fact—to change. While they're not required to report on what they do about climate or greenhouse gas emissions or sustainability or social responsibility, many do, partly because so many of their stakeholders care. The Securities and Exchange Commission (SEC) does have guidelines—and only guidelines, for now—for reporting direct and indirect risks and opportunities related

---

[22]Center for American Progress. (2013). "The Arab Spring and Climate Change: A Climate and Security Correlations Series." *Center for American Progress,* February 28, (2013). https://www.americanprogress.org/issues/security/report/2013/02/28/54579/the-arab-spring-and-climate-change/; The Earth Institute Columbia University. (2015). "Did Climate Change Help Spark the Syrian War? Scientists Link Warming Trend to Record Drought and Later Unrest." http://www.earthinstitute.columbia.edu/articles/view/3235 Study: http://www.pnas.org/content/112/11/3241.abstract.

to climate change,[23,24] but regulations down the road may encourage companies to attend more carefully to their emissions.

Yet publicly traded companies are under increasing pressure from multiple stakeholders, including investors, to report on sustainability as issues like climate that are seen as potential business risks. Indeed, a number of companies have been reporting for going on a couple of decades. The result is a proliferation of sustainability data and reports, but no consistent measure by which to benchmark performance among companies. Indeed, what a company voluntarily reports in this arena is to a large degree self-determined, which can lead to public reproaches of "'greenwashing."

In this context, what a "leader" is within any sector remains difficult to determine. While groups like CDP (formerly Carbon Disclosure Project) request businesses disclose information like GHG emissions and climate change risks and opportunities, among others, companies have no obligation to do so.

The Sustainability Accounting Standards Board (SASB) developed in recent years from the confusion in sustainability reporting; it aims to set up standards within industries, often grouped somewhat differently from more traditional groupings (like the Global Industry Classification Standard (GICs[25]), that can help securities analysts and investors compare

---

[23]Ceres. (2016). "Cool Response: The SEC & Corporate Climate Change Reporting." Accessed January 4, 2016. https://www.ceres.org/resources/reports/cool-response-the-sec-corporate-climate-change-reporting/view.

[24]The US Security and Exchange Commission's (SEC) new guidance for including climate change risks in corporate disclosures includes a focus on water risks. Although corporate reporting related to climate change issues is often limited to energy and emissions data, the SEC's guidance includes looking at exposure to impacts of climate change like water scarcity, and salt water intrusion from rising sea levels. The new guidance may have a global impact in the form of a "ripple effect" along a business' supply chain, as firms subject to SEC regulation require similar reporting from their suppliers and distributors. However, this may also mean heavy reporting requirements for businesses. "US Securities & Exchange Commission (SEC) Guidance Regarding Disclosure Related To Climate Change—Ecosystem Marketplace". (2016). Ecosystem Marketplace. http://www.ecosystemmarketplace.com/resources/us-securities-exchange-commission-sec-guidance-regarding-disclosure-related-to-climate-change/.

[25]GICS "seeks to offer an efficient investment tool to capture the breadth, depth and evolution of industry sectors. It is a four-tiered, hierarchical industry classification

peers, in a format that is familiar, with information that's "material" to the industry, or likely to affect a company's financial condition or operating performance. A more recent initiative, the Task Force on Climate-related Financial Disclosures (TCFD), announced by the Financial Stability Board during the COP 21 in Paris in December 2015, aims to set guidelines on climate disclosure.[26]

Climate is an issue SASB considers cross-cutting, in that it affects multiple industries; the group estimates it affects in some form 72 of 79 industries it has examined, though what might be relevant to investors varies by industry. Significantly, SASB's founder and CEO Jean Rogers noted that the current state of disclosure on climate is often "rudimentary . . . boilerplate information in statutory disclosures, often noted as a risk factor but nothing really useful for an investor."

Given the rudimentary state of disclosure, it's perhaps unsurprising that "industries doing more on disclosure are farther along in understanding their contribution to the problem and future scenarios of how to address it," Rogers said, and that "sectors not disclosing or disclosing boilerplate information are the ones behind in understanding how it affects their performance." She added that it's an "important leading indicator of where some industries are in preparing for resilience."

In my years of studying individual companies across sectors and their sustainability and climate initiatives, I've observed a similar trend: generally, those interested in disclosing and discussing their progress are, again,

---

system. It consists of 10 sectors, 24 industry groups, 67 industries and 156 sub-industries. Companies are classified quantitatively and qualitatively." "In 1999, Standard & Poor's and MSCI Barra jointly developed GICS to establish a global standard for categorizing companies into sectors and industries. GICS was developed in response to the global financial community's need for one complete, consistent set of global sector and industry definitions, thereby enabling asset owners, asset managers and investment research specialists to make seamless company, sector and industry comparisons across countries, regions and globally." Global Industry Classification System: Real Estate". (2016). MSCI. www.msci.com/gis/.

[26]The Task Force will engage a wide range of stakeholders in setting recommendations for "consistent, comparable, reliable, clear and efficient" climate-related disclosures by companies. The TCFD is set to deliver recommendations for voluntary disclosure and leading practices by the end of 2016.

those leading the pack. The companies profiled in the chapters to come fall into that category.

Yet, despite the continued complexity of comparing industries and companies, a growing body of companies—even fossil fuel companies at the heart of the GHG problem (and not treated in this book)—are now requesting that government "put a price on carbon." In other words, they acknowledge that it's not "free" to emit GHGs; that there are "costs" (consequences to the public good, to the public's health, to a functioning world, among others) that should be counted, just as other costs and liabilities are counted—and accounted for—in P&L statements and acknowledged in balance sheets.[27]

For instance, in spring 2015, a group of powerful European fossil fuel companies, including BP, Total, Statoil and Shell, requested that the UN help them devise a carbon pricing system.[28] Such action may lead eventually to carbon taxes or to more working and workable carbon markets that trade carbon credits as a means of reducing GHGs.

Of course, the picture isn't all rosy. There are challenges to moving forward and creating positive change. Many of these are quite ubiquitous throughout organizations of all sorts, businesses included. But the challenges present opportunities, too. And many challenges are quite simple both to identify and to fix—once the will is there, with the collaborative spirit and promise of the right reward.

Why Companies Care about Resilience

Not infrequently, a company's work toward climate resilience originates with a long-standing, skilled sustainability team that has gained the respect

---

[27]This June, six oil and gas companies urged governments to put a price on carbon. "We firmly believe that carbon pricing will discourage high carbon options and reduce uncertainty that will help stimulate investments in the right low carbon technologies and the right resources at the right pace," said chief executives of BP, Royal Dutch Shell, BG Group, Eni, Statoil and Total. "Six Energy Companies Call For Carbon Pricing". (2016). Phys.Org. http://phys.org/news/2015-06-energy-companies-carbon-pricing.html.

[28]The Financial Times. (2015). "European Energy Groups Seek UN Backing for Carbon Pricing System." May 31, 2015. Accessed August 17, 2015. http://www.ft.com/intl/cms/s/0/2fc5662e-0643-11e5-b676-00144feabdc0.html#axzz3j59HZzbh.

of the executive suite—and often throughout the company —as well as the organizational savvy to see its suggestions through. Partly that's because traditionally, subjects like climate change have been the bailiwick of the sustainability team. And when the team has garnered respect throughout the organization, often over a long period of time, it's more likely to have the clout to bring its ideas on climate and resilience to those who can help actualize them. That's why so many of the executives interviewed for this book are part of their company's sustainability, environmental, health, and safety (EHS), or related teams.

What's more, as risks proliferate, there's greater awareness that more disruptions could occur at any time, and hence greater concern for preparedness and prevention. And, once something happens that affects the company directly (or even indirectly), management is more likely to view resilience as a priority—in a world where multiple changes vie for immediate attention—and to begin to prepare for the future, as well as to prevent future crisis and loss. That's why some US-based companies began to address resilience after Hurricane Katrina 2005, while others were alerted during the Sendai earthquake and tsunami in 2011, and still others awakened after experiencing serious supply chain interruptions during the 2011 floods in Thailand. Of course, Hurricane Sandy in 2012 was an unavoidable wake-up call for US-based companies. Current climate trends, notably drought in the western US, are affecting increasing numbers of companies.

The chapters in this book, briefly outlined below, profile the emerging approaches some leading companies are taking to climate resilience. As the chapter titles belie, they represent five principles that others could adopt, molding them to their needs and aims: *Responding to Weather, Learning from Disaster, Doing More with Less, Taking a Risk and Managing It, Communicating Change and Collaborating for Resilience.*

i. Responding to Weather (Chapter 1)

One notable example of a company affected by severe weather is Citibank (in Chapter 1), along with many of its clients. Citi's Wall Street headquarters was caught in the thick of Superstorm Sandy's wrath. In the midst of the hurricane, power was out, basements were flooded, and millions of dollars were lost. The bank, which has long been a sustainability leader, put the experience to good use. Its resilience response: Citi is building more redundancy into its systems, changing the placement of data bases that were in basements, fortifying its buildings to LEED Platinum standards. While the bank was already improving energy efficiency, it has doubled down. What's more, Citi is using new energy financing techniques developed for its own facilities to create similar products for its customers.

At the simplest level, the bank responded to a severe weather event. At a more sophisticated level, the bank's respected sustainability team was able to help drive a larger plan. That plan brought together operations and risk management functions to develop a new market, as well as new financing possibilities to lessen wider dependence on fossil fuels. Another positive result: The bank was able to forge better understanding of climate and renewable energy in different functional units (e.g., operations, risk management, and sustainability), as it built support for its new energy initiatives, improved communications and fostered collaboration among traditionally disparate silos.

ii. Learning from Disaster (Chapter 2)

Sprint, as a telecommunications provider, is another company that has experienced first-hand crises worsened through inadequate or nonfunctional communications. The company also has effectively incorporated lessons learned into its emerging resilience approach, in part guided by its highly-regarded sustainability team, which has relied on good relationships with other functions within the company (notably, the emergency response team) to drive climate-awareness initiatives.

As a strategic utility, the telecom provider is on the front lines during disasters so it must be deft at both responding to emergencies and at learning—often fast—from past crises. Its experiences during Katrina, the Missouri River floods, hurricane Sandy, as well as its Japanese parent company Softbank's experience of the tsunami, have put Sprint on high alert.[29]

That means that what the company learns must lead to preparation (e.g., through back-up power generation, among other actions) for potential hazards known or still unknown.

---

[29]"Year-Round Business Continuity Preparations Ensure Sprint Nextel Is Ready For 2006 Hurricane Season | Sprint Newsroom." (2016). Sprint Newsroom. http://newsroom.sprint.com/news-releases/year-round-business-continuity-preparations-ensure-sprint-nextel-is-ready-for-2006-hurricane-season.htm.

And that's what the company does on a consistent, regular basis: It takes stock of what it has learned and updates—often and quickly. Quick responsiveness to Katrina is testimony to that. Sprint is now using some of those lessons creatively, to introduce customer-facing telecommunications services for what it views as an increasingly uncertain climate.

iii. Doing More with Less (Chapter 3)

Perhaps no industry is more familiar through experience with the potentially devastating effects of supply chain interruption than the agriculture and food sector, which is on the front lines of climate change and stands to bear huge potential losses from it, spanning farm to table to waste disposal. So it's perhaps unsurprising that food companies are preparing for both sudden events and longer-term trends related to climate change with emerging resilience approaches throughout their operations—from increased communications and collaboration with farmers, to trimming waste in production facilities, to improving energy sources, lightening the haul, and shortening the distance of food transport.

As in other industries, the combination of adapting to climate change, while mitigating it by cutting emissions (e.g., through more efficient production and transportation, as well as waste reduction) can also lead to innovations that create new markets for new products. What's more, doing more with less (reducing transport, energy, and waste) throughout the supply and value chain itself helps to boost the company's resilience to climate by lowering its exposure to risk. For instance, by shortening and lightening hauls, ConAgra and Stonyfield not only cut costs but also reduce the risk of transport interruptions during weather events that might otherwise prevent food from reaching consumers.

iv. Taking a Risk—and Managing It (Chapter 4)

Perhaps no sector is more familiar with risk—taking risks and managing them—than the insurance industry, exemplified here by The Hartford. Climate change is a risk in itself, one that a company has to assess and manage and one that affects other risks. Indeed, the World Economic Forum ranked extreme weather events the second most likely risk in 2015, just after interstate conflict.[30] In terms of impact, water crisis ranked number one, while failure of adapting to climate change was rated 5th out of 28 risks. And, according to insurance experts in 2015, top risks include business and supply chain interruption as the first, with natural catastrophes rated second.[31]

Climate change begets change, and change is intrinsically risky. As the sector that helps protect others from risks they're bound to take, insurance necessarily adopts a broad look at risk, mainly because that's how the business makes a profit. Hence managing risk well becomes a priority.

However, even as The Hartford manages risk, it also takes risks, some of which—at least in the climate arena—have already paid off. For instance, it was one of the first in the United States to "take the risk" of insuring renewable energy projects, a growing market from which the company stands to profit.

Likewise, the company took the risk of creating new insurance products that incentivize its customers to take steps to fortify resilience and reduce GHGs—like offering better insurance rates on hybrid or electric vehicles. Finally, the company has taken the risk (or, perhaps, precaution) of testing the waters of some of these moves on itself—before offering them to its customers. Examples include incentivizing its own employees to drive electric vehicles by offering charging stations at the company's facilities, which reduces the company's indirect GHGs.

v. Communicating Change, Collaborating on Climate (Chapter 5)

Indeed, a frequent barrier to developing a climate resilience approach is inadequate collaboration, often due to insufficient communication.[17]

That challenge, as well as how it may be overcome, is highlighted in the last chapter that recounts IBM's approach to one county's climate

---

[30]World Economic Forum. (2015). "International Conflict Tops List of Global Risks in 2015." Accessed January 4, 2016. http://reports.weforum.org/global-risks-2015/press-releases/.

[31]Allianz. (2015). "Allianz Risk Barometer: Top Business Risks 2015." Accessed January 4, 2016. http://www.agcs.allianz.com/assets/PDFs/Reports/Allianz-Risk-Barometer-2015_EN.pdf.

challenge through the company's Smart Cities program. Many steps to resolving the challenges of communicating change aren't hard; they're just not used as much as they should be.

For instance, encouraging different branches of county government to actually converse can lead—and in this case did—to learning that information one branch already has may be useful to another. That, in turn, can lead to collaboration, which can lead to community engagement, including business engagement.

Updating systems can help identify data gaps or duplications, make information compatible and easier to share. All this—data review and streamlining, systems updates, and, especially, information sharing—can help ignite community engagement, which is critical to preparing for potential climate crises and preventing worst-case scenarios, including those affecting lives and livelihoods. The same insights apply to business.

Climate Change, Business Change

What these companies have in common is an awareness of climate change, a willingness to do something about it, and some ideas of how to prepare in order to survive and even thrive as the climate continues to change. More important, their innovative spirit in the face of potentially frightening shifts reminds us that we're built to make changes, often improving conditions and lives. The business changes outlined here have the potential to make money. What's more, they have the potential to do good. In other words, the changing climate is beginning to inspire positive business change.

CHAPTER 1

Responding to Weather

Citi's Climate Resilience Plan: Energy, Operations, and Risk Management

What a difference a year can make.

In February 2014, after the Federal Reserve rejected Citigroup's capital plan as part of the regulator's post-2008 financial crisis "stress test," the nation's third-largest bank announced an ambitious three-point strategy to deal with a likely increase and intensity of climate-related events worldwide. After all, the bank, like other firms headquartered on Wall Street, had suffered dearly during Superstorm Sandy some 18 months earlier. Plus, with operations in over 160 countries, Citi must think globally.

In its 2013 Global Citizenship Report, released in early 2014, the bank wrote that 3 years ahead of schedule, it had surpassed its 10-year goal of directing $50 billion to "activities mitigating climate change, including financing for renewable energy and energy efficiency and investments in the greening of Citi's operations [and] met our 2015 operational environmental goals for greenhouse gas and waste two years early, reducing our emissions by 25 percent."

Then just one year later in March 2015, the bank, for the first time in years, passed the Fed's stress test for its capital plan. And Citi's CEO, Michael Corbat, announced that the bank was adopting an even more aggressive sustainability goal: a 10-year commitment to "lend, invest and facilitate $100 billion . . . for projects ranging from energy, to clean tech, to water, to green infrastructure," twice the amount of its previous investment.

In that ambitious plan, Citi reiterated—while buttressing—its three-pronged resilience approach, which includes financing energy efficiency and renewable energy projects, reinforcing its operations and supply chain to prepare for potential interruptions, and expanding its risk management activities.

Importantly, the plan, spearheaded by the sustainability team early in the first decade of the millennium, is part and parcel of Citi's business plan, as Corbat stressed in introducing the latest version of the bank's goals. Corbat explained:

> These efforts do not constitute philanthropy, nor do they represent costs. In fact, they reduce costs—and also increase revenues, enhance client relationships, and help manage risk. In other words, these efforts are integral to Citi's business strategy.

Sandy's Wake-Up Call

Citi's 2015 announcement came two and a half years after some of the bank's operations in New York City had been badly affected by Hurricane Sandy. Just over a year after the storm, the bank had already taken important steps to update some facilities, notably those in the Wall Street area, to prepare for future extreme weather events.

Citi, long a sustainability leader, awoke to the growing threat of climate change in the aftermath of the storm, a turning point in public—and corporate—awareness of the looming crisis. The bank's 2015 announcement showed Citi's determination not just to prevail in the face of potential threats, but to excel and innovate in the climate arena—not only for the sake of its continuity as a business and the safety of its employees and the communities in which it operates, but also for the good of its customers. The bank's new commitments, while solidifying its intention to reduce greenhouse gases (GHGs) to mitigate climate change, also include new products and services to help both individual and institutional customers adapt to a changing climate, some first tested on Citi's own turf to prove their mettle. The creative efforts are particularly noteworthy in an industry that can be slow to take the lead, particularly since the economic crash of 2008.

Nonetheless, despite its ambitious climate goals, Citi continues to carry climate risks. Like other big banks, it provides financing to large carbon dioxide (CO_2)-emitting clients in the coal industry. Citi got a 95 for disclosure in the 2013 CDP S&P 500 Climate Change Report. While the score didn't qualify the bank for that year's Climate Disclosure Leadership

Index, covering open disclosure of climate change mitigation and related activities, the bank ranked far higher than the average of 79 for financials.[1]

When it comes to support of fossil fuel projects, where there's smoke, there may be fire—as an Exxon report, released in 2014 discussing the risks of that company's potentially stranded oil and gas assets, made clear. That kind of stress could come home to roost at Citi, as at other firms, if shareholders start to voice concern, although Citi does work with groups like the Coalition for Environmentally Responsible Economies (CERES) and the Environmental Defense Fund (EDF) on such issues. The bank is strengthening its risk management policies to avert growing risks, and its ambitious resilience plans could help to offset any alarms. Indeed, as of 2015, a retiring Citi executive pointed out that some of the leading fossil fuel producers are also taking the lead in moving toward renewable energy.[2]

Perhaps most important, the bank's 2015 report highlights a case the year before where the bank declined to finance a US fossil fuel project, suggesting a shifting attitude toward such activity:

> In 2014, Citi considered taking an equity stake in a large operational coal-fired power plant in the United States. The facility had a sizable unlined coal ash storage pond, which is not considered best environmental practice, and had been subject to allegations of contamination of the local groundwater. Coal ash contamination has generated much public debate in recent years, and in late 2014, the EPA finalized a rule to update national coal ash disposal requirements.[3]

While the plant met all current governmental regulations, Citi ESRM (environmental, social, and risk management) felt that the transaction

---

[1]CDP: Driving Sustainable Economies. (2013). "Sector Insights. What is Driving Climate Change Action in the World's Largest Companies?" Accessed August 15, 2015. https://www.cdp.net/cdpresults/cdp-global-500-climate-change-report-2013.pdf.

[2]Makower, John. (2015). "Inside Citi's Plan to Deploy $100 Billion for Cities, Renewables, Climate." *Greenbiz*, February 28, 2015, accessed August 11, 2015. http://www.greenbiz.com/article/inside-citis-plan-deploy-100-billion-cities-renewables-climate-solutions.

[3]Citi. (2014). "2014 Citi Global Citizenship Report." Accessed August 11, 2015. http://www.citigroup.com/citi/about/data/corp_citizenship/2014-citi-global-citizenship-report-en.pdf.

represented outsized environmental and franchise risk and declined to give approval.

Citi's refusal to fund the project augurs well for more such moves in the future. Still, a major shift can take time. While many argue that the pace of adapting to a world already witnessing radical climate-related changes may not be optimal, even relatively swift moves in this arena aren't immediate. As Bruce Schlein, Citi's Director of Alternative Energy Finance, remarked about the bank's recent updates to some flagship energy projects, they have taken a couple of years to come to fruition. "Anything new doesn't happen at the same pace as what we've been doing for years. It takes longer, partly because there are lots of different market actors inside and outside [the company] who need to get comfortable" with innovations, such as new energy financing projects and mechanisms. Such projects also involve working among sectors, including different levels of government, which can be domestically especially in a highly regulated industry—and even stickier for a bank that operates globally. That is particularly true of collaborative initiatives among for-profit companies, NGOs, and government entities—sometimes called public–private partnerships (PPP)—as are some of the firm's energy efficiency efforts designed to help reduce carbon and other emissions from energy sources.

Energy Financing

Among the three prongs of Citi's ambitious sustainability plan, energy finance is emerging as one of the most innovative. In announcing Citi's ambitious new goals in 2015, CEO Corbat noted:

> Citi has financed some of the largest renewable energy projects in the world, including the Solar Star photovoltaic project in Southern California for Berkshire Hathaway Energy in 2013, the largest single renewable energy project finance bond offering to date. This project is expected to generate 579 megawatts of power when it is completed by the end of this year, making it the largest solar project in the world. Solar Star is expected to provide enough energy to power more than a quarter million homes, with

the electricity generated displacing approximately 570,000 metric tons of carbon dioxide.[4]

Among other renewable energy projects in 2014, Citi also supported SunEdison with a $160 million facility "to finance a pool of distributed generation solar projects for commercial and industrial properties in the United States, averaging 1.1 megawatts each. The facility utilizes a structure that provides tax equity for roughly 40 projects,"[5] according to the 2014 report.

Corbat added that the bank is "targeting reductions of 35 percent in greenhouse gas emissions, 30 percent in energy and water use; and 60 percent in waste." The long-term ambitious goal is to reduce GHGs by 80 percent by 2050.

In addition to its leadership on renewable energy projects and its ambitious goals to reduce GHG emissions, Citi also has advanced significantly in two areas of energy efficiency financing: one aimed at the single-family residential market, in which the bank has two noteworthy projects (Warehouse for Energy Efficient Loans, or WHEEL, and Kilowatt), and another for corporate and industrial properties (Green Investment Bank, or GIB). The bank organizes its work in energy efficiency according to property type, mainly because of differences in how financing is structured based on ownership, Schlein explained.

Of its flagship corporate energy financing project, Citi's London project with the UK's British GIB, Corbat said:

> We're innovating not just on the types of projects we finance, but also the way in which we finance them. For instance, this past November we sought outside funding for an operational improvement—a move that many might not expect a financial institution to make. We developed an innovative energy efficiency measure to cut energy

---

[4]Citi. (2015). "CEO Michael Corbat Delivers Remarks on Citi's $100 Billion Commitment to Finance Sustainable Growth." Accessed January 4, 2016. http://www.citigroup.com/citi/news/executive/150218Ea.htm.

[5]Citi. (2014). "2014 Citi Global Citizenship Report." Accessed August 9, 2015. http://www.citigroup.com/citi/about/data/corp_citizenship/2014-citi-global-citizenship-report-en.pdf.

use by 10 percent at our London data center. Using a first-of-its-kind financing structure, the project is being funded through these energy savings and it involves no upfront capital from Citi. This is a model that's applicable and attractive to clients of all types, and one that we expect to use more and more going forward.

Citi's energy efficiency project at its data center in London is the first of its kind at a UK data center and the first project in the financial services sector to be to be backed by the UK's GIB. GIB invested £2.6 m in the £5.2 m project.

As part of the project, Citi installed a Combined Cooling and Power (CCP) system that generates over 70 percent of the center's electricity, while cooling the servers located there. Previously, Citi's London data center got its electricity from the national grid, with back up from diesel generators. The project, expected to cut the data center's energy use by 10 percent while reducing GHGs, included adding a CCP plant and other efficiency measures in the air handling and conditioning equipment. IT is among the most energy-intensive industries, second to aviation, with energy accounting for as much as 80 percent of the cost of running a data center, according to Shaun Kingsbury, Chief Executive of the UK's GIB.[6]

The GIB project, in the works for many years, is unique mainly because Citi, instead of self-financing the project as is done conventionally, is both the property owner and the debt provider. Instead of using its own operating capital for capital improvements, the bank used third-party financing, including GIB as an equity investor, and the bank itself—"Citi lending to Citi," Schlein said. The project's financing structure is especially noteworthy in that "most, if not all" of corporate America uses self-financing for energy improvements to operations, setting a payback period of 1½ to 2 years, after which many have exhausted their willingness to pay, he added. Once the financing threshold has been reached, the company has three options, Schlein explained:

---

[6]Green Investment Bank. (2014). "UK Data Centre to Cut Energy Usage in First of a Kind Project." Accessed August 9, 2015. http://www.greeninvestmentbank.com/news-and-insight/2014/uk-data-centre-to-cut-energy-usage-in-first-of-a-kind-project/.

The first is to stop, and no one wants to do that, because we're all setting more aggressive greenhouse gas reduction goals. A second option is to change the threshold to look at three or five years or longer, and the issue with that is that energy isn't a core part of the company's business—the company isn't in the business of funding energy projects, even if it's the foundation of the business. So, if you're trying to decide between business extension in China or retrofitting buildings, and the first is more core to the business, you choose the former. The last option is seeking a third-party solution, a provider who's in the business of energy services or energy finance to do it and figure out a way to have them finance it.

In London, Citi wanted to set more ambitious goals in energy improvement, and, because the bank isn't an energy services company, it didn't make sense to allocate more capital to the project. Instead, "we used ourselves as a guinea pig, going through all the steps to figure out how to procure energy as a service, transitioning from a mode of operating that we're comfortable with, where we self-finance—to looking for a third party. In that process, we decided we wanted to be able to offer it as a financing product for clients," an innovative approach that would include a test run with Citi as provider.

Innovation and Collaboration

After the London deal closed at the end of 2014, providing "an opportunity for our operations and banking teams to learn from each other and collaborate on something," two key things happened, Schlein said:

> Now our operations team is looking at the model as something they can use at a larger scale. And, on the banking side, the team is in dialogue with clients they can tell about the financing product that makes so much sense, we even did it ourselves.

In other words, the innovative project not only will save Citi money and cut its greenhouse gas emissions, it also served as a chance for two "silos" in the company to work together and learn from each other about a growing business, while creating a model of how to do it; the bank can now sell a new financing product to other companies that increasingly need and want it. What's more, Citi, as its own client in this project, now has an example for itself to emulate, and, indeed, plans to replicate it at facilities elsewhere.

Schlein emphasized that the London project offers "new ways for different parts of the company to work together and benefit mutually," often an amorphous goal in a global company with nearly a quarter million [241,000] employees—and a vital step in improving any company's resilience strategy. As the deal was approved from committee to committee throughout the bank, over 30 people collaborated on the project extending their knowledge of energy efficiency as well as financing.

He added that the bank's sustainability team—on which he served before moving to energy finance—initially proposed the idea to the operations team, demonstrating the critical role sustainability can play in raising a company's awareness of the importance of climate resilience and its many benefits, including cost reductions, while prodding the company along the process.

WHEEL Gets Energy Efficiency Moving

On the single-family energy efficiency financing side, CEO Corbat highlighted WHEEL and Kilowatt Financial as "game-changing projects the bank is looking to do more of," explaining that these are national platforms that support loans for home energy efficiency improvements:

> We financed the projects in 2014 and have been working with state and local governments—including Florida, Indiana, Kentucky, New York, Pennsylvania, and Virginia—the federal Department of Energy, and several nonprofits, to facilitate adoption of a new approach that opens the door to institutional investors. These platforms have so far served more than 6,700 households.

Announced in 2014, the WHEEL plan, in conjunction with partner Renewable Funding, propels the bank further along its climate resilience path in the area of single-family energy efficiency financing. WHEEL backs state energy efficiency loans, using public funds to lower the interest rate of the loans, thereby reducing investors' risk and decreasing the cost for homeowners.

WHEEL followed on the heels of the Kilowatt project announced in early 2014. With for-profit partner, Kilowatt Financial, Citi financed a $100 million debt facility, pooling loans to allow homeowners to make energy efficiency improvements at a far lower rate by securitizing the pooled loans in the capital markets.

"What's significant about these deals is that they help establish energy efficiency as an asset class, facilitating the flow of more and cheaper capital to energy efficiency and greater potential for scale," Schlein said. That eventually translates into lower carbon emissions.

With single-family energy efficiency financing initiatives, Citi's goal is "to help scale energy efficiency, in this case with single-family homes, by serving as the [financial] intermediary—filling a gap between investors, who can bring cheaper capital to this, and programs that need access to capital," Schlein explained. "We're bridging the gap by functioning as the intermediary that aggregates loans and puts them into a size and format that makes them investible" for institutional investors. Citi was the first bank in the United States to house and securitize unsecured consumer energy efficiency loans to homeowners (as opposed to PACE—Property Assessed Clean Energy—which secures loans via property taxes and also offers renewable-energy financing).

While homeowners have been trying to increase energy efficiency for some time, Citi—and others—offer them an opportunity to do so by securitizing the loan. Explained Schlein: "We're helping to create energy efficiency as a new asset class, like student or auto loans, for institutional investors that want to deploy capital into efficiency." And while state and local efficiency programs for homeowners have existed for some time, WHEEL is the first time loans from these programs are being aggregated and securitized—providing programs and homeowners with access to better sources of capital. Again, as in other steps along the resilience path, this has taken time: Citi began engaging with WHEEL stakeholders in 2010, and in 2014 established a warehouse facility to purchase loans out of state and local programs. "For a year we've been purchasing and aggregating the loans, so that they can get to a size and format required by institutional investors, including analytics and due diligence on the portfolio, to demonstrate it is investible."

A year later in 2015, Citi was already "deep into step two," Schlein said, which is the first securitization of both WHEEL and Kilowatt. "Those will be really significant, because in WHEEL, it's states that join the platform," he explained. What's more, WHEEL is the first facility to aggregate and securitize unsecured energy efficiency loans.

The first to adopt the program were Kentucky and Pennsylvania, and, since then "others, like New York, have to differing degrees stated their intent to join," Schlein said. "Part of getting them to the next step is showing them proof of concept, that we can deliver benefits, channel [loans] to institutional investors [with] ability to access more efficient capital."

What's important about the nascent market that's "moving from successful pilots at the state level to a scale that other states can adopt," Schlein said, is that it creates "a positive, virtuous cycle that emerges, because you start a flow of more and cheaper activity." That means that, as individuals have easier access to loans to finance energy efficiency in their homes, the institutional investors, who help finance individuals' cheaper access to capital, also profit from their investments.

Sandy's Wake-Up Call for Operations

Citi's approach to climate resilience also includes managing its own operations to ensure they can run under environmental stress. Those operations, on which consumers, businesses, and international relief agencies rely for money to pay for invaluable resources like water, must endure even worst-case scenarios.

Hurricane Sandy brought into vivid relief the potential vulnerability of operations,[7] explained Chris Magliano, who heads Citi's global critical facilities group from Brazil. "Climate does play a role in the way we locate and build our facilities," said Magliano:

---

[7]Darrell, Andy. (2013). "What New York's Sandy Success Can Teach Us About Resiliency." *Greenbiz*, January 18, (2013), accessed January 18, 2013. http://www.greenbiz.com/blog/2013/01/14/New-York-Sandy-resiliency.

Sandy is a perfect example. The New York-area facilities were heavily affected, and we've learned a number of lessons. One of our key facilities in downtown Manhattan, 111 Wall Street, was flooded with over a meter of water, shut down, and out of commission. It was damaged to the point where it couldn't be reopened for over six months. That building houses a couple thousand employees, mostly working in technology.

And we had other facilities in the line of fire. Our building at 390 Greenwich Street houses a big data center and trading operations. The place could run, but we had flooding in the basement and water right up to the edge of the building. Our data center in New Jersey located near a river likewise had water infiltration.

Magliano manages Citi's portfolio of real estate housing technology—everything from large data facilities down to smaller server rooms—all over the world, setting standards for how the company builds and operates critical facilities.

One lesson from Sandy is that where equipment is inside the building may be as important as where the building itself is situated:

The loss of 111 Wall Street and other impacts elsewhere opened our eyes to be better prepared next time to new and existing conditions. From a facilities and infrastructure perspective, one thing we would do differently is we don't want to have all infrastructure in the basement. All our electrical switch gear is there, and we had over a meter of water, which destroyed all the utilities switch gear. It cost millions in damages, and reconstruction was in the tens of millions. So we're trying to elevate those.

We're also considering how to better prevent water infiltration. 111 Wall Street already had flood gates in response to a Nor'easter that had flooding effects. Afterwards, Citi installed sort of submarine barriers, on the lower sides of the building near NYC's East River. And in the basement we installed submarine doors with inflatable tubes to keep out the water and make a seal.

Even so, "too much water went over the tops of those gates [during Sandy]," Magliano said.

Buildings, Energy, Supplier Engagement, Emission Cuts

To ensure against such risks in the future, in New York and at its more than 12,000 facilities worldwide, Citi is bolstering operations and supplier guidelines in its 2015 strategy. The bank set its "third generation of environmental footprint goals," said Val Smith, Director of Corporate Sustainability, including reducing water use by 30 percent, and waste-to-landfill by 60 percent by 2020. Citi also set "a new green building target for 30 percent of our facilities worldwide to be LEED certified," she explained. The bank's aim to make its headquarters in New York Leadership in Energy and Environmental Design (LEED) platinum certified, applying for certification after renovations are completed. That move should help Citi reduce its own GHG impact. Said Citi's CEO, Corbat:

> We've pledged that by 2020, a third of our real estate portfolio will be LEED Certified—meaning that they meet exacting environmental standards. As of now, 253 of our sites around the world hold this distinction. Soon, there will be an important addition. We will seek the highest level of certification—LEED Platinum— for the renovated 388-390 Greenwich Street, which will become our new, consolidated global headquarters.
>
> LEED Platinum is, to say the least, very hard to achieve for a renovation—for buildings constructed long before most of these new standards came into being. It involves getting inside the structure's skeleton and "guts" and changing much of its physical plant. Setting such a goal for this building is ambitious but, we believe, the only choice worthy of our firm's continuing aspiration to be the world's greenest bank.[8]

Perhaps even more ambitious, Citi now aims to cut energy use at its facilities worldwide by 30 percent (from a 2005 baseline), again by 2020. With GHG emissions, the bank took a different approach altogether. "In studying our greenhouse gas reduction target, we took a new approach

---

[8]Citi. (2015). "CEO Michael Corbat Delivers Remarks on Citi's $100 Billion Commitment to Finance Sustainable Growth." Accessed January 4, 2016. http://www.citigroup.com/citi/news/executive/150218Ea.htm.

based on an emerging discussion of climate science-based goals," Smith explained, in line with results from the latest Intergovernmental Panel on Climate Change (IPCC) report published in 2014 indicating the need to limit GHG emissions and keep the global average temperature increase to below two degrees Celsius, Smith said.

"Using this goal as our framing, we developed our target [cuts] by looking at our contribution to global GDP, our global footprint and the distribution of our facilities, using the framework from the UN IPCC report," a process several other companies have also adopted, she noted. Based on those factors, Citi now targets a 30 percent decrease of GHGs by 2020 and an 80 percent decrease by 2050, she explained, adding: "All the work we've done and targets set on data center consolidation, green buildings, greenhouse gas and water reduction are all in the climate resilience space."

In a related move, Citi set new goals for supplier engagement and supply chain policy, which includes three priority categories: paper, IT hardware and E-waste disposal, and, most closely related to GHG cuts, travel and logistics. Citi's focus on these three areas, Smith explained, arose from:

> a combination of our understanding of which key areas in our supply chain are most important to our operations and level of spend. And we engaged with our stakeholders to learn what some of the issues of importance are to them, laying out three strategic priority areas, including climate change, sustainable cities, and people and communities. We also engaged with our suppler engagement team, just as client engagement is central to our risk management approach.

Risk Management Extends to Environmental and Social Risks

That risk management approach, critical to Citi, as to so many companies—in a world with increasing risks that are more easily communicated than ever before—took on more urgency in light of the effects of Sandy on the bank itself and its clients. Still, at its core, the approach is rooted in the Equator Principles, which Citi, and a consortium of banks, launched in June 2003.

The Equator Principles "are the core of our environmental and social risk management policy," said Smith, "and they're important because they're industry wide, so they're the rising tide of all boats. They cover standards for specific sectors and areas of special focus. This is the approach we take for project finance and for corporate loans, where we know what our financing is going to," she says. Expanded requirements of the Equator Principles III, which Citi applied to its 2015 goals, cover strengthened risk management on climate change, among other points.

"The expertise in environmental and social risk management we build up at Citi is something we offer our clients," she continued, with two new areas of review: first, conducting portfolio-level review of higher risk, carbon-intensive sectors; and second, developing a system to analyze emerging risks, including issues like development activities in the Arctic, water stress and availability in different geographic areas, and how various industries are working for zero net deforestation. "Implementation and continuous improvement of our ESRM policy is fundamental to our approach with clients," Smith said. "Going beyond that, we look at how to strategically address this with portfolio-level analysis and in a targeted way to monitor emerging risks," she added.

As key examples, the bank's combined experience of Sandy in its own operations and its work in energy efficiency and developing new asset classes has informed its environmental and social risk management strategy to better understand clients' potential risks, especially in sectors considered particularly vulnerable.

"Our own direct operations experience with disasters and technology expertise helps inform both the products/services and risk management buckets," said Schlein. "That experience makes it real and helps the organization understand the ramifications and how it would be important to our clients," especially as a lender in New York.

That first-hand experience reflects "what's happening in the financial sector broadly," said Courtney Lowrance, Director of the Environmental and Social Risk Management Team, which is part of the bank's overall risk management division.

Her team reviews transactions that come with environmental and social risk. "Climate has been a hot topic in the past few years, and since Sandy it's been even more elevated," Lowrance continued.

She added that, since most banks have similar teams, they collaborate on emerging issues, such as climate adaptation or resilience, through initiatives such as the Equator Principles or the United Nations Environment Programme (UNEP) Finance Initiative.

"One challenge historically is that the [environmental impact assessment, or EIA] documents don't include a robust risk assessment of climate change. Financial institutions are trying to change that," said Lowrance. "The consulting sector writing the EIAs [could] take a two-step process to include climate risk. One is they can use global climate models that are statistical models that the IPCC draws on, and develop scenarios for project site and sea levels in the future." But that's not part of current practice now, "mainly because historically the focus has been on the impact of that project on the environment, instead of the impact of the environment on the project," as comes with climate risk. "We're making progress, but there's a lot to be done," Lowrance said:

> Since Sandy, one thing we've been doing that's new is looking at portfolio-level reviews of particular sectors. Some sectors have higher vulnerability to climate change, especially the building sectors in coastal areas, agriculture and power and energy, which rely on water input, and so are especially vulnerable to climate change, as in the southwest U.S., where there's a drought.

Lowrance added, "As an environmental specialist, I think it's important to look at natural infrastructure and the services it provides. So if a building is going up on the coast, I'd want to see that dunes or other natural structures stay in place," as protection.

"We hope that through environmental impact assessments, we can change not just the design [of a project] but also ensure that services provided by habitats or natural environments are more integrated into project design." The social risks from climate also must be evaluated. She explained:

> Part of what we look at in an EIA is a description of ecosystem services provided at the project site. Those are systems nature provides to people. If you impact those ecosystem services, you impact human populations. So one thing we look at is communities near a project, and we evaluate two things: first, dependence of

the communities on those services—for instance, do they depend on the river for drinking water? And secondly, does the project depend on those services? If a power project is [built] on the river, will it compete with people's needs in terms of water?

So we definitely look at the social issues as well, and that's mainly through the lens of ecosystem services. That will become more important as people become more aware not just of climate change but also of the services nature provides.

Much of Lowrance's work is in the developing world, where Citi also has operations and portfolios. "We see the most vulnerability to climate change in the poorest countries. I think they have to build the resilience of those poor places and often don't have resources to do that. And part of resilience is protecting the environment."

She added: "In my view, the best solutions are natural."

Conclusion

The three hallmarks of Citi's plan—attention to energy, operations/supply chain, and risk management—might well serve as a useful template for how a number of leading companies could approach resilience in the face of a changing climate.

Sandy

Dramatized by the effects of Hurricane Sandy, especially in the wake of previous disasters whose effects were felt globally throughout the business world—including the earthquake and tsunami in Japan in 2011, Typhoon Haiyan in the Philippines in 2013, Hurricane Katrina in the Gulf Coast in 2005—the risks to companies of not buttressing operations and supply chains were brought into painful relief, serving as a wake-up call to many companies to plan for resilience.

Adapt, Mitigate

As Citi's 2015 intensified goals show, pursuing resilience as an adaptive strategy isn't a substitute for reducing greenhouse gas emissions to mitigate climate change. The two are complementary. Indeed, Citi has set even more ambitious GHG reduction goals in its latest plan.

Strengthening Operations

Part of Citi's adaptive strategy will be accomplished by buttressing operations at facilities worldwide—for instance, by ensuring the bank has redundant data systems and better locations within those facilities—a critical step for all companies these days, as they rely increasingly on such systems to do business.

Energy

Another part of the resilience plan will be accomplished by cutting energy use, which reduces Citi's GHG emissions. In Citi's case, its own energy cuts and experimental financing approach are leading to the creation of new energy financing mechanisms and markets.

Managing Risk

Citi is extending its own reinforced, and still-evolving, internal environmental and social risk management plan to support clients in their own risk management, even as the bank continues to beef up its standards for applying project finance to various sectors (partly based on their climate risk).

Innovation and Business Opportunity

Notably, these latter two targets—energy reduction and increased risk management—have proven to be opportunities for the bank to create new business opportunities for itself, even as it addresses its clients' needs and responds to the pressing world problem of a changing climate. As Citi's CEO Michael Corbat said in introducing the latest version of the bank's goals:

> These efforts do not constitute philanthropy, nor do they represent costs. In fact, they reduce costs, and also increase revenues, enhance client relationships, and help manage risk. In other words, these efforts are integral to Citi's business strategy.

Communication, Collaboration

Finally, Citi has managed to create these business opportunities partly by ensuring that stakeholders—often internal teams as different as facilities management and banking, or external clients or other banks—communicate, collaborate, and learn from each other. The bank's new energy financing mechanisms as well as its revised and reinvigorated risk management approach, to be used internally and externally to help clients, are other examples of collaborating for innovation. The communication and collaboration help to educate employees and strengthen relations with clients and other external stakeholders.

CHAPTER 2

Learning from Disaster

For Sprint, Communication Is Core to Climate Resilience

Like so many large, multinational companies, Sprint has undergone its share of corporate challenges and changes in the face of global economic woes, customers' downsized pocketbooks and shifting tastes, along with increased demands for short-term profits from so-called activist investors, among others. For Sprint, such pressures have been especially elevated since 2013, when Japanese telecommunications company SoftBank Corp. bought 80 percent of the company for $21.6 billion, with the idea of a merger with T-Mobile to take on rival wireless carriers AT&T and Verizon.[1]

When SoftBank announced it wouldn't pursue T-Mobile in August of 2014, Sprint's parent company also appointed a new CEO. Already a Sprint Board member, Marcelo Claure, the Bolivian founder of Brightstar—an international distributor of wireless products and services, owned by SoftBank—was charged with turning the carrier around financially.[2] As Sprint strived to improve its network after SoftBank acquired it, the company lost customers and saw its stock price drop dramatically. By August of 2015, the company had slipped to last place among the four US carriers, prompting CEO Claure a few months later to pledge budget cuts of up to $2.5 billion in the following 6 months.

---

[1]Farrell, Maureen. (2014). "SoftBank's Tough Times at Sprint." *Wall Street Journal*, November 11, 2014, accessed November 11, 2014. http://blogs.wsj.com/moneybeat/2014/11/11/softbanks-tough-times-at-sprint/

[2]Carlyle, Erin. (2014). "Sprint's New CEO, Marcelo Claure Of Brightstar, Is Worth $900 Million." *Forbes*, August 6, 2014, accessed August 6, 2014.http://www.forbes.com/sites/erincarlyle/2014/08/06/sprints-new-ceo-marcelo-claure-of-brightstar-is-worth-900-million/#9a728155770e

Yet, even as Sprint has undergone ownership and leadership transitions, a massive cost-cutting campaign, and a slide to fourth place in the industry, its commitment to sustainability and related climate resilience measures have earned it accolades over the years. Those include: the Environmental Protection Agency (EPA) Corporate Climate Leadership Award, Wastewise Partner; the EPA Champion Award and Gold-Tier Participant in the EPA Sustainable Materials Management Electronics Challenge for leading the way in collecting and recycling electronics; the EPA Sustainability Leadership Award in 2012, in recognition of its climate-sensitive E-waste management program; 2014 EPA's Climate Leadership Award for Organizational Leadership and Supply Chain Leadership 2014 for influencing their supply chain and continually focusing on reducing greenhouse gas emissions; Compass Intelligence Eco-Focus Mobility Awards in 2014; and repeat inclusion on the Dow Jones Sustainability Index North America (2011–2015). Sprint is also the only US telecommunications company that belongs to World Wildlife Fund's (WWF) Climate Savers Program and Coalition for Environmentally Responsible Economies (CERES).

The carrier's early recognition of the dual need to lower its emissions and those of its suppliers, while building an increasingly resilient system in the face of mounting climate conditions may prove to be a competitive advantage. As Sprint has worked to improve its network, ensuring more innovative, resilient infrastructure, it has almost simultaneously been learning from one emergency to the next how to build preparedness into its emergency response operations, so necessary for a society—from businesses to government to individuals—increasingly reliant on telecommunications to carry out.

As emergencies, many generated by weather-related events, happen more frequently, people everywhere are increasingly turning to smart phones to guide them. And, we're all ever-more reliant on multiple forms of social media to communicate with each other, especially during emergencies. Behind the scenes, more data is being collected, sorted, and analyzed, and people expect to have it at hand when it's needed—not least in volatile situations. What's more, data culled through social media interactions is now more actively adapted to help alert communities to potential threats, while so-called citizen scientists are also encouraged to gather and communicate such information (see IBM chapter).

As a telecommunications company, Sprint must stay on top of such trends. What's more, the carrier must factor in the reliance that others—individuals and institutions—place on the continuity of its operations, which, in extreme situations, can become a matter of life or death both for network users and the company. With the growing occurrence of climate-related disasters growing, Sprint sees climate readiness as a critical aspect of its sustainability practice, explaining in part why it has focused its sustainability and climate resilience activities on ensuring network continuity.

Emergency Learnings

Indeed, when it comes to climate resilience, Sprint continues to ready itself for uncertainty. Such climate-ready activities, rapidly becoming part and parcel of the carrier's sustainability initiative, aren't likely to be hurt by cost cuts—partly because they are proving at Sprint, as elsewhere, to lower costs.

The principle of preparing for increasing uncertainty in the face of intensifying weather volatility and severity is particularly visible in the company's emergency-response operations, which are continually tweaked. In what surely is a glaring understatement, Tanya Jones, manager of Sprint Corp.'s vital Emergency Response Team (ERT) Operations, observed, "We learned quite a bit from Hurricane Sandy."[3]

Like all telecommunications carriers, Sprint lost cell sites on the northeastern seaboard and in New York City in the 2012 superstrom, which hurt its cellular operations. Fortunately, Sprint's ERT was able to provide critical communications services to first responders and emergency agencies using COWS (Cell On Wheels) and COLTS (Cell on Light Trucks) vehicles, including near the World Trade Center in New York, where they were parked in front of the Freedom Tower.

Among the key learnings from the debacle, said Jones: how better to rebuild, where better to stage, and perhaps most important, how better to "future-proof our technology to ensure our equipment is upgraded and our personnel equipped" for disaster.

---

[3]LaMonica, Martin. (2013). "One Year Later, Hurricane Sandy Fuels Grid Innovation." Greenbiz, October 24, 2013. https://www.greenbiz.com/blog/2013/10/24/one-year-later-hurricane-sandy-fuels-grid-innovation.

Her team of disaster emergency workers in multiple U.S. locations, including Dallas and Sterling, Va., is at the center—and on the front lines—of Sprint's emerging approach to climate resilience. Overseeing the company's disaster response for 10 years and finding herself on the spot during 2,500 events—from hurricanes to fires to tornados to floods—Jones' interpretation of such events is telling.

A Communications Approach to Resilience

Jones' thoughts on disaster and climate echo the observation of Sprint's Director of Corporate Responsibility and Sustainability, Amy Hargroves, who spearheads the company's climate resilience approach: "The same risks exist for climate-related events as for other disasters, but there's a greater range of events and more of them." Of acute importance, Hargroves noted: "In our field, as a communications company, disaster resilience has to be core to our business, because there's so much dependence nationally on communications." While majority owned by Japanese SoftBank, Sprint's network is United States-centric, serving federal, state, and local governments as well as emergency responders—and, of course, the company's 50 million-plus business and individual customers.

Because emergency response is at the core of Sprint's resilience approach, the company is always at the cutting edge of communications technology: "LTE, high-speed data, 4G, emergency response—we can provide that now, but most of what we do is make sure we're on top of technology, because it's not if but when a disaster will happen," Jones explained.

Keeping its ERT up to date with special equipment and mobile communications—as well as learning from each disaster—is only one part of Sprint's four-pronged approach to implementing climate resilience, a business priority of Hargroves' award-winning sustainability team.

Other priorities in Sprint's resilience approach include the following:

- Frequent assessments of the company's network risks (with higher risks assessed quarterly until they're no longer classified as high).

- Improving backup power with less carbon-intensive sources, including research on hydrogen fuel cells, in part with the Department of Energy.
- Often reviewing lessons learned to find new business opportunities, including those related to customer offerings.

Overarching goals include reducing the company's greenhouse gas emissions and electricity use by 20 percent by 2017 (from 2007 levels) and ensuring 90 percent of its supply chain meets Sprint's environmental and social criteria. Sprint's 150 largest suppliers account for the company's biggest environmental impacts and 90 percent of its sourced supply chain expenditures. As of 2015, nearly 80 percent of Sprint's supply chain met its environmental and social criteria.

The key to meeting the environmental and social goals was twofold—reducing GHGs and electricity use. It was through Sprint's massive network overhaul that was completed in 2015, Network Vision—at a cost of nearly $5 billion over three years—that allowed Sprint to achieve its goals.

Partly because suppliers account for a large portion of its environmental footprint, Sprint provided free guidance on GHG measurement, reporting, and reduction strategies to its top suppliers, including those involved in the network overhaul. The process of GHG measurement is now so complicated that it had become off-putting to suppliers, many of which, as smaller operations, don't have the resources to master the process that a company of Sprint's size and breadth—or that of some of the carrier's multinational suppliers, such as Apple—has to understand for sustainability reporting, measurement, and materiality assessment factors.

Because the company's cost reductions won't affect the network side of the business, this guidance is likely to continue to prove useful in reducing Sprint's Scope 2 emissions.[4] To ensure continuing emissions reductions in line with its 90 percent goal, the company is also developing

---

[4]The GHG Protocol Corporate Standard classifies a company's GHG emissions into three "scopes". Scope 1 emissions are direct emissions from owned or controlled sources. Scope 2 emissions are indirect emissions from the generation of purchased energy. Scope 3 emissions are all indirect emissions (not included in scope 2) that occur in the value chain of the reporting company, including both upstream and downstream emissions.

a responsible sourcing council within its supply chain organization, assigning a relationship manager to each category of supplier to develop expertise that can be applied to the company's frequently changing set of suppliers.

Network Risks: Cell Sites, Signaling, Fleets, Response Prioritization

To ensure the network stays up to date—and up and running—in case of disaster, the company runs quarterly risk assessments.

Key network risks include the following:

Fleets: The company's fleet of vehicles for a range of conditions could affect the cell sites, the most vulnerable part of the network. However, Hargroves noted that Sprint's fleet, with 1,200 vehicles, has a substantially smaller GHG footprint than those of its direct competitors, which have 40,000 or more vehicles.

Cell sites: With some 55,000 cell sites across the country, Sprint has a lot to keep track of. The signal from the site must be accessible in order for wireless customers to complete calls. Cell site traffic is aggregated at over 100 major satellite switching sites that allow calls to be terminated between various wireless and wireline networks. Much of the IP-based (Internet Protocol) control functionality is handled by some 30 core sites that act as traffic directors for voice and data services. With rapidly changing network structure and technology, the number of cell sites are expected to increase in 2016.

Fortunately, Hargroves noted, insurance companies have been building climate risk into their corporate risk models, assessing the level and nature of risk per site. With that information, Sprint can determine which sites may be most vulnerable or which may be candidates for relocation, considering 500-year flood levels when rebuilding its sites. "Networks are complicated beasts, and risk varies according to [each] site," said Hargroves. "But the most important parts to protect are the switch sites, mainly because they aggregate traffic from thousands of cell sites. A single switch outage can isolate a complete market, leaving customers without critical wireless services over a large geographical area."

Emergency response: Of growing importance to the company's resilience plan is the sort of emergency response to disasters that Jones manages. "We anticipate greater demand for the services of our ERT because of the increase in the number of disruptive events," Hargroves explained.

Essential to the response is the specialized mobile equipment, such as mobile communications centers, including COWs and COLTs. These vans or trailers are especially useful in places that are hard to access. "Demand for COWs and COLTs has increased over the past several years, so our fleet has been [growing] and is expected to continue to grow," she explained.

A big part of emergency response is sequencing and prioritization: That entails determining who is "in charge" of disaster management (from a government perspective), which communications capabilities are intact and which are needed—and then developing a prioritized list of communications services and infrastructure that the company will provide during a disaster.

Sprint may send out its ERT to work with government and provide initial critical communications services for first responders—government personnel, military, FEMA (Federal Emergency Management Agency), and Red Cross—to enable them to communicate, especially if primary infrastructure, such as cell site towers, signal repeaters, or switching centers, has been disabled. The Sprint ERT always works with local government, including sheriffs and firefighters. Next in line are customers.

Risk, Site Planning, and Backup Power: Response to Storms, Fires, Flooding

While Sprint always has had backup power initiatives, they have expanded throughout the United States over the past few years—as has the need for backup, which has grown with the frequency of disasters. Yet, despite the broad expansion of backup services, the company has managed to reduce electricity costs by more than a third.

"Provision of backup power is very much motivated by both natural and manmade disasters," said John Holmes, formerly Sprint's Manager of Network Planning, responsible for the company's strategic planning efforts involving backup power, energy efficiency, and sustainability for the company's network. The need for backup power varies by region. Holmes explained:

> In the eastern and southern coastal regions, hurricanes and tropi-
> cal storms can cause widespread damage. In the Midwest and
> upper Midwest, ice storms can result in widespread outages. Wild-
> fires can be a problem anywhere there's a combination of very dry
> weather and a lot of combustible ground or tree cover. As a general
> rule, they are more frequent out West. Places like California or the
> Pacific Northwest are susceptible to earthquakes.
>
> Also, don't count out tornadoes. Heavy rainfall can result in
> flooding, and many times that will occur downstream of where
> the majority of the rainfall occurred.

Sometimes the power stays on, but Sprint "can still have widespread outages if say, a major backbone fiber carrying multiple backhaul circuits (which connect the BTS[5] equipment to the switches) is cut," Holmes pointed out. "That would prevent calls from being completed . . . and is often manifested to the wireless subscriber as a fast busy signal."

What's more, Hargroves added, the question of where to build cell sites has been complicated by the increase in frequency and severity of storms, as well as the availability of energy and water sources.

"A few years ago, we studied the impact of climate change on water scarcity and cost in the U.S. The results were shared with the C-suite and operational teams so they could use it as input for site planning. For instance, if you need a big building, you should expect it to have a water chilling system, which is a big driver of water use. If you know where water will be scarcer, and thus more expensive, you should avoid building in those areas," Hargroves explained.

She added that given California's ongoing drought and water use re-duction mandate, "it's reasonable to expect water costs to further increase, changing the ROI for water projects there."

In 2013 and 2014, water cost the company about $1.2 million, com-pared with $300 million for energy in 2013, which rose to $333 million

---

[5]Base Transceiver Systems facilitate wireless communication between users and the network.

in 2014, "so it's a far lower economic priority," she said. "However, given the importance of water globally, it would be foolish not to consider drought forecasts in your site-planning process."

Hargroves noted that "reassessments occur frequently—and substantive changes in cost options are a trigger for program re-evaluation," as could be the case for California, for instance. However, she added that "the total costs will still be relatively low, since our energy costs are nearly 300 times our water costs."

By contrast, Sprint has a strong economic incentive to reduce its energy usage, which is primarily electricity. By the end of 2014, the company used 40 percent less electricity than 7 years earlier, resulting in cost savings of $168 million. Including Clearwire, acquired—along with its emissions output—in 2013, Sprint's electricity costs are still down by 19 percent.

Power Backup and Hydrogen Fuel Cells

When disaster strikes, electrical power from traditional sources is likely to go down, as recent climate-related events, including Superstorm Sandy, have shown. That's why backup power is essential for telecommunications providers like Sprint. A backup plan is needed for all critical components in the network. Because Sprint is committed to decreasing GHG emissions, the company looks to cleaner backup power sources. The combined need for both consistent and clean backup power led the company to hydrogen fuel cells, which, in turn, helped to reduce GHG emissions by nearly half.

"Our second priority for carbon reduction is backup power, which is a leading contributor to Sprint's Scope 1, or direct, emissions," said Hargroves. By 2014:

> Scope 1 emissions represented only 4.5 percent of our aggregate Scope 1 and 2 emissions. Within the 4.5 percent, 12 percent is emissions from backup power sources, such as diesel fuel and propane.
>
> Sprint includes its Scope 1 emissions in its goal to absolutely reduce GHG emissions by 20 percent by 2017, and in fact, had reduced them by 43 percent by 2014. Increasing our use of hydrogen fuel cells and propane—and decreasing use of diesel generators—as backup power sources at cell sites has contributed to this success.

The company's sustainability goals were set in 2008 by Sprint's then CEO, Dan Hesse, based on recommendations of the corporate responsibility team, who initially suggested a GHG reduction goal of 12 percent. The CEO upped it to 15 percent, and then increased again to 20 percent after the carrier announced its Network Vision plan.

"When we talk about network resiliency, we mean the ability of the network to maintain power and functionality, particularly at the switching and cell site level," she said. If primary power fails, there are several backup power options that are used. These include diesel generators, natural gas feeds, even propane and methanol. In each case, the backup options are able to support multiple electricity streams in a single place to provide backup power. While solar and wind power are used where possible, neither technology is practical given risks (when wind is strong, a disaster could be in the making), lack of continuous availability of energy, and cost-benefit balance. When it comes to minimizing risk of losing backup power, Hargroves explained:

> There are multiple lines of defense, the first of which is batteries. Since we have the greatest dependency on batteries, much of our focus is on reducing the environmental impact and duration of use of our network batteries. We have partnered with the National Renewable Energy Lab and the Department of Energy on battery technology, which is so critical for a communications company.

Sprint maximized its use of hydrogen fuel cells in part through work with the DOE, whose $7.3 million grant in 2009 supported the company's development and deployment of 260 additional fuel cells to support its backup power systems, former network planning manager Holmes said.

The innovative fuel cells use an on-site, refillable, medium-pressure hydrogen storage system, which has eliminated bottle swaps (required in earlier generations of the technology), while boosting the standby runtime of the cells to parity with that of other backup solutions such as diesel generators. The company's 500-plus hydrogen fuel cells help Sprint ensure that its Scope 1 emissions related to backup power stay low despite significant increases in network resilience, achieved via more sites with longer backup power.

The main challenge with fuel cells is difficulty of refueling. Also, hydrogen tanks take up a lot of space, which is not ideal at some sites. That has led the company to explore many fuel-efficient options, including natural gas, propane, and methanol.

Customers and Business Opportunity

One business opportunity in climate resilience for the company is on the consumer side of the business, said Hargroves. "We're trying to identify additional services we can provide to help customers" understand and prepare for potentially disruptive events. Due to ongoing changes at the carrier, a recent focus is on digital inclusion, including providing free mobile connectivity to the Internet for low-income youth (the company is providing free wireless data access to 50,000 such students) in an effort to help close the digital access divide.

So far, most of the company's focus has been on the "survivability of network infrastructure," Hargroves said. The company's Japanese parent SoftBank has exceptional experience in this arena, gained during the Great East Japan earthquake of March 2011.

Explained Hargroves:

> Up to now, the main things we've done involve the survivability of our services—directly helping first responders, supporting customers on billing, and managing our service—versus providing information that can help them manage through the disaster; [this is] things like how to extend the life of your phone battery, recharge with limited electricity sources available—which is different from relaying information during a disaster—as people become more and more dependent on cell service.

But the company imagines the opportunity to change that. Sprint may have a competitive advantage in consumer engagement, if it can leverage some other assets of SoftBank such as Yahoo (in Japan) and provide disaster-related content on its customers' phones.

She added: "We do think there are some interesting opportunities with emergency alert systems and disaster content support. So if someone can figure out a good way to do it, this is a terrific opportunity."

Indeed, she noted that, while the company has been a key supporter of the Amber Alert system that helps locate missing children, there are equally important services yet to be developed for disasters and emergency situations. Such solutions will likely be featured in the company's ongoing sustainability strategy. She added: "Disaster communications is very relevant to the power of communications companies to help society. We're working to identify our opportunities to most significantly impact society in a positive way."

Conclusion

Telecommunications in a Changing Climate

As a communications company, Sprint is on the front lines of technology, communications, extreme weather and climate, disasters, emergency preparedness—and, perhaps most important, of providing a vital service to the public.

Acknowledging such risks for the telecommunications industry as a whole, the US General Services Administration (GSA), released a report in November 2014 entitled *Climate Risks Study for Telecommunications and Data Centers*, prepared by Riverside Technology, Inc. and Acclimatise, warning:

> Telecommunications and data centers are key utilities sectors that facilitate the functioning and connectivity of the United States economy. Disruptions in the ability to communicate or access information severely inhibits governments, companies, and citizens, and in periods of disaster or extreme events, this inability to communicate puts national and human security and business value at risk. Climate variability and change may threaten the infrastructural integrity and productivity of these critical sectors, increasing the number and severity of disruptions. Extreme or unusual weather can lead to cascading impacts felt across sectors and borders.[6]

From its experiences of disaster—during Hurricanes Katrina and later Sandy, as well as during the Missouri River floods in 2011—Sprint has taken precautions to future-proof its infrastructure at cell and switching sites to stay at the cutting edge of technology and prepare for emergencies. Moreover, the company incorporates risk assessment into its regular

---

[6]Adams, Peter, Jennifer Steeves, Brian Ashe, John Firth, and Ben Rabb. (2014). *Climate Risks Study for Telecommunications and Data Center Services*. Fort Collins: Riverside Technology, Inc., p. 5.

operational practices. Sprint's review of process risk additionally informs business opportunities to help customers prepare for disruptions, which is simultaneously an extension of the social good—namely, vital communications services—the company provides. Finally, Sprint's climate resilience approach has largely been part of its overall strategy for sustainability and directed mainly by Sprint's sustainability leadership, ensuring that its risk assessment addresses social and economic concerns.

Sprint is a smaller player in a brutally competitive industry. It has undergone ownership and leadership transitions and is in the middle of a massive cost-cutting campaign. Nonetheless, it recognized early on the need to both build a system increasingly resilient to the changing climate and to lower GHG emissions in its own facilities as well as in its supplier networks.

Learning From Disaster

It's easy in principle, harder in practice: learn from experience, especially the unfortunate experiences of disaster. Sprint has built its experience from disaster into preparation for it in several key ways: readiness for emergencies; continual learning and risk assessment; risk management and business continuity, partly through adaptation, partly through mitigation; and seeking business opportunities for positive social impact.

Preparing For Emergencies

Sprint's experiences during disasters continue to help the company learn how better to rebuild, where better to stage, how better to future-proof its technology, how better to ensure its personnel are equipped for the inevitability—if uncertain timing—of emergencies. Sprint's focus in emergency preparedness, as with other parts of its resilience approach, is on continual learning and building those lessons into the process of emergency management.

One aspect of continual learning on the part of personnel is ensuring collaboration between ERT and those responsible for updating the network infrastructure, as well as those responsible for the overall resilience strategy—namely, the sustainability leadership. In other words, practicing internal communications helps to assure that the communications company can do its job—namely, guarantee its communications for its customers.

Continuous Learning and Risk Assessment

Learning from more frequent and intense disasters has helped Sprint adopt a widespread culture of continuous learning and frequent risk assessment, in a sector whose vulnerability to disaster is particularly acute and whose value chain—its customers throughout society including emergency workers outside the company itself—rely on communications service availability in order to effectively respond to disaster. Continual learning can mean that scheduled risk assessments may not be enough—and that whenever a disaster occurs, individuals who assess risk at all levels in the company participate in the review process. This forges a virtuous cycle of continuous learning and collaboration in company-wide risk management.

Business Continuity—Adaptation and Mitigation

A critical part of Sprint's risk assessment is managing the risk of power outages, the threat of which rises with the increase in frequency and intensity of sudden weather events, like hurricanes, and ongoing climate crises, like droughts. Enhancing its network infrastructure, especially its switching and cell sites, to ensure backup against the risk of outages, is one way the company is ensuring business continuity—before, during, and after disaster. Bolstering backup power sources, a way of adapting to climate change, has led the company to rethink its energy sources and develop backup systems that use multiple fuels or alternatives like hydrogen fuel cells. Turning to renewable energy sources is a way of mitigating future climate change by reducing greenhouse gas emissions. This kind of thinking—preparing for the risk of business interruption by looking at the climate risks posed by natural resources the company uses—is also informing Sprint's placement of infrastructure, especially in areas experiencing ongoing drought.

Business Opportunity, Positive Social Impact

The company's climate resilience approach, which has been housed mainly with its sustainability leadership, is expanding to other business functions and shifted to many teams as the sustainability group turns toward internal functions. As Sprint becomes more aware of disaster preparedness throughout the company, opportunities for new business and positive social impacts have become a secondary effect. In Sprint's case, where emergency readiness is core to the company's business continuity and resilience approach, that positive social impact suggests opportunity in helping alert customers to potential extreme weather and related climate events. The learning that Sprint's parent SoftBank experienced—and any subsequent customer offerings in the form of disaster warning content through the 2011 earthquake and tsunami in Japan, may help Sprint to find new ways to serve its US customers, build awareness, and prepare for potential emergencies.

CHAPTER 3

Doing More with Less

Part I: How ConAgra Sets the Table for Climate Resilience

Like other big food producers, ConAgra has come under mounting financial pressure, as Americans increasingly consume less processed food. And, like other major brand favorites, including Kraft and Heinz, which merged in 2015, the company has been looking to cut costs to stay competitive. So it came as little surprise that ConAgra announced plans in October 2015 to cut $300 million from its annual budget.[1]

Yet, even as it looked to tighten its belt, the manufacturer of brands like Chef Boyardee and Hunt's tomato sauce also announced a plan to work with more than 250 other giants, including General Mills, Kelloggs, and Chipotle—in conjunction with the EPA and the US Department of Agriculture—to halve food waste by 2030. Because food waste accounts for almost 20 percent of the potent greenhouse gas (GHG) methane released in the U.S. annually, the pledge could have a significant effect on national emissions reductions.[2] The agriculture and food industry account to 30 to 40 percent of global GHG emissions according to FAO estimates,[3] while 40 percent of food produced becomes waste.[4]

---

[1]Gasparro, Annie. (2015). "Next Step For Conagra: Streamlining Its Supply Chain." WSJ. October 2, 2015. http://www.wsj.com/articles/next-step-for-conagra-streamlining-its-supply-chain-1443829529.

[2]Grady, Barbara. "ConAgra, Albertsons, Sodexo join fight to half food waste." GreenBiz. (September 18, 2015). https://www.greenbiz.com/article/conagra-albertsons-sodexo-join-federal-fight-halve-food-waste

[3]FAO. (2016). "Agriculture's Greenhouse Gas Emissions On The Rise". FAO.Org. http://www.fao.org/news/story/en/item/216137/icode/.

[4]Gunders, Dana. (August 2012). NRDC. "Wasted: How America Is Losing Up To 40 Percent Of Its Food From Farm To Fork To Landfill."

Since 2010, $16 billion ConAgra, which is moving its headquarters from Omaha to Chicago as part of its cost-reduction measures, has already diverted at least 75 percent of its solid waste from landfills, in the process boosting food donations to charities, improving technology, shifting to more sustainably sourced food production, and cutting costs—along with GHG emissions.

To provide healthier food without stoking climate change, the company has been executing a four-pronged resilience approach since adopting its first set of sustainability principles in 2010, when it became clearer that changes in climate would affect all aspects of its business, from farm to table and beyond:

1. Implementing energy efficiency strategies throughout its facilities to achieve a GHG reduction goal of 20 percent per pound of product by 2020, drawing heavily on employee engagement[5] and strategic capital investments in facility infrastructure, such as boiler control system upgrades, heat recovery projects, and lighting retrofits;
2. Working with supply chain partners to assure long-term, sustainable sourcing of ingredients through high standards for agriculture practices and transport efficiency;
3. Fine-tuning a corporate climate change policy;
4. Eliminating food waste in its facilities, thereby reducing the amount of waste sent to landfills and, by extension, cutting the resulting GHG emissions.

Climate Risk and Resilience: Manage, Mitigate, and Monitor

ConAgra recognizes that climate change is expressed both by sudden, sporadic, extreme weather events—such as Hurricane Sandy in 2012, or the Missouri River floods in 2011—as well as ongoing extreme conditions, such as the California drought.

---

[5]Nagappan, Padma. (2012). "ConAgra Foods' Green Strategy: Award Employees for Sustainability Efforts." *GreenBiz*. May 10, 2012. https://www.greenbiz.com/blog/2012/05/10/conagra-foods-employee-engagement-key-to-green-success

Both affect the company's business, though in different ways. During and after Sandy in 2012, the company had to act quickly to protect its employees and facilities, while implementing business continuity plans to minimize interruptions in production and service to customers. Both Sandy and the Missouri flood required considerable flexibility in the company's operations—within its own facilities and with its suppliers—according to Marcella Thompson, ConAgra Foods' former Director of Sustainability in the company's Environment, Health & Safety Department.

Meanwhile, ongoing climate conditions result in stress on agriculture, which means subsequent pressures on the company. Situations like long-term drought and fires underscore the importance of maintaining long-term relationships with farmers, the fundamental supplier for a food company. This is especially critical in areas hard-hit by dry conditions and water scarcity over a period of years, such as California, where farmers grow tomatoes for ConAgra's two fresh-pack and canning facilities. In these cases, the company must look increasingly to farmers to adopt best practices to conserve water, while maximizing yield.

Food Waste

Intensifying weather conditions have also increased ConAgra's concern about the deep connection between climate change and food waste, which food companies can no longer ignore. In 2013, the agricultural sector, through crop cultivation, accounted for 10 percent of U.S. GHG emissions.[6] Also, considering that up to 40 percent of food grown and prepared is never consumed, the company was able to identify an opportunity to mitigate climate change simply by eliminating waste. The challenge extends up and down the supply chain, starting at the farm and extending all the way to plate waste in homes and restaurants. Once in landfills, food waste produces GHGs, further exacerbating the problem.

In its Fifth Assessment Report, the Intergovernmental Panel on Climate Change (IPCC) estimates that about a quarter of global GHG emissions are due mainly to "deforestation, agricultural emissions from soil

---

[6]Agriculture Sector Emissions. (2016). US EPA. Retrieved 13 July 2016, from https://www3.epa.gov/climatechange/ghgemissions/sources/agriculture.html

and nutrient management, and livestock."[7] The Food and Agricultural Organization (FAO) of the UN in its 2013 Food Wastage Imprint summary report estimates that about a third of food produced for human consumption is wasted. The FAO goes on to estimate that "the direct economic cost of food wastage of agricultural products (excluding fish and seafood), based on producer prices only, is about USD 750 billion, equivalent to the GDP of Switzerland."[8]

Stress to food production systems will likely increase as the world is faced with feeding nine billion people by 2050, ConAgra estimates. In this context, "Resiliency means everything is on the table—beginning with how and where food is grown, to what and how much people eat," explained Thompson.

Viewed from this perspective, the company's quest to find ways to deal with climate change through adaptation and mitigation measures is essential. That's why, in 2010, ConAgra included in its first set of sustainability goals diverting at least 75 percent of waste from landfills to more productive purposes, such as donations, animal feed, energy recovery or composting (for organic materials), and recycling (or energy recovery for packaging).

"In very short order, we realized that we needed to have a strategy to manage these material streams not as wastes but as by-products that still had value," explained Gail Tavill, ConAgra's Vice President of Sustainability. "Shifting our attitudes about these materials left over from manufacturing really helped several of our facilities take action."

In an effort to reduce GHGs by eliminating food waste at landfills, the company put systems in place in 2012 to track landfill and material diversion from its facilities, identifying 15 waste categories in line with the EPA's waste reduction model. The results include improved understanding of the GHG emissions from the company's management of

---

[7]IPCC, (2014). Summary for Policymakers. In: *Climate Change 2014: Mitigation of Climate Change. Contribution of Working Group III to the Fifth Assessment Report of the Intergovernmental Panel on Climate Change* [Edenhofer, O., R. Pichs-Madruga, Y. Sokona, E. Farahani, S. Kadner, K. Seyboth, A. Adler, I. Baum, S. Brunner, P. Eickemeier, B. Kriemann, J. Savolainen, S. Schlömer, C. von Stechow, T. Zwickel and J.C. Minx (eds.)]. Cambridge, UK and New York, NY, USA: Cambridge University Press, 2014. p. 24.

[8]FAO. *Food wastage footprint: Impacts on natural resources. Summary Report,* (2013). p. 7.

waste materials, as well as the ability to quantify benefits from diverting them from landfills to "higher-value homes."

ConAgra estimates that in 2013 it diverted 93 percent of waste materials from landfills, avoiding more than 165,000 metric tons of GHG Scope 3 emissions.[9] By fall of 2015, the company had exceeded its goal, sending less than five percent of organic materials to landfills as waste, while continuing to reduce waste overall. In 2013, ConAgra announced a 2020 vision for sustainability, including a goal to reduce the amount of waste it generates by one billion pounds by 2020.

From Waste to Profit

Significantly, ConAgra has also learned that cutting waste can increase profit. At the company's frozen pie dough plant in Council Bluffs, Iowa, ConAgra employees tracking waste found that the facility was generating more than 2,000 pounds of dough waste daily.

They identified the main source of waste as Pie Line 3. To prevent dough overhang, a new form of block was installed, cutting the dough waste by 60 percent, or 235 tons annually. What was formerly waste is now sold as product.

In a similar case, employees at ConAgra's pudding factory in Waterloo, Iowa created a whole new market from what had been a vast waste stream. They watched for years, as tasty, though blended—and hence unsellable—pudding was produced, as one flavor changed to another on the production line—and eventually was dumped as waste.

Thanks to a cross-functional team seeking to cut waste, the blended pudding is now packaged and sold to correctional facilities, which generates profit in addition to eliminating over 1,000 tons of food waste (more than 20 percent of total waste for that factory), while cutting waste disposal costs and yield loss by 15 percent.

Employee Engagement

As these waste-to-product cases show, ConAgra employees are key to identifying opportunities to cut waste, finding innovative solutions,

---

[9]See Chapter 2 Footnote 4

and implementing new procedures and policies. Active Green Teams in most company locations are a central part of ConAgra's employee engagement strategy. Supported by plant management, the teams foster collaboration among hourly employees across multiple disciplines and shifts.

Green Teams operating on the spot have demonstrated they are critically positioned to identify opportunities to cut waste and make other improvements to reduce GHG emissions and boost sustainability within ConAgra's facilities. Explained Thompson: "Our employee Green Teams bring our sustainability ambitions to life. They are the heart and soul of our program."

Some basic training is the first step. "Initially, we had to educate our team on what GHGs are and our past performance, so that they could understand and communicate to others about our goals," said ConAgra's Continuous Improvement Specialist, Debbie Stanley. "After understanding GHGs, [employees] were excited to help develop solutions that could impact the goal."

"The hardest part has been putting in the time and resources to ensure employees understood GHGs. Yet the rewards of employee engagement have been considerable," she explained. "Several times a week, I have team members come up with energy saving ideas and solutions and bring them to Green Team members, and I've had Green Team members lead projects to reduce GHGs."

When ConAgra wanted to improve the company's energy efficiency policy, it turned to the Green Teams. To get employees on board with energy efficiency, ConAgra's frozen food facility in Russellville, Ark. held a Green Day during Earth Month in 2014. The local Green Team led activities to raise awareness and engage employees, hosting games such as "Spin the Wheel" to help participants learn energy facts, and a dice game to answer questions on key resources for the facility—electricity, water, and compressed air.

The payoff has been substantial, ranging from decreasing utility costs for the facility to boosting employee enthusiasm for the measures. "We've made [Green Teams] a big deal by really recognizing those who helped implement sustainability projects," said Stanley. "Generally they're eager to make a bigger difference."

At ConAgra's potato facility in Warden, Washington, the Green Team created the "What's a Picture Worth?" program to encourage employees to look for opportunities to cut waste, with the aim of raising awareness of "everyday waste" and reducing waste overall.

The Green Team split into three groups, each charged with a different goal: one looking to cut energy waste, another to cut water waste, and a third to find recycling opportunities. Each group was given a camera to take photos of waste throughout the plant to be shared with all team members.

The exercise generated 70 potential ways to cut waste.

Climate Resilience in the Supply Chain

One issue of critical importance to ConAgra's approach to climate resilience, as for many others in the food sector, is how best to work with its supply chain, which—from farming to packaging to transportation—is highly diverse and complex.

"It is important for us, and other companies, to understand our supply chains to assure long-term access to materials and minimize risks," said Tavill. As an example, she cited the company's sustainable agriculture programs that focus on those crops "where we have direct relationships with farmers," including potatoes and tomatoes. "It's the direct, long-term relationships we have with these business partners that enable us to collaborate effectively to really drive change."

For instance, the company has helped its potato growers put into practice more water-efficient irrigation practices, which reduces GHG emissions by cutting electricity use from pumping water. Many farmers have implemented water conservation best practices, which include using soil moisture probes to direct irrigation only where needed and identifying dry spots with aerial infrared technology to then employ low-flow, drop-down sprinkler nozzles in order to apply precisely the right amount of water.

"Our farmers and Ag Services team have taught me that there's both an art and a science to farming," explained Thompson. "Innovative application of technology in agriculture enables farmers to grow more food on less land—with far fewer resources."

ConAgra has thousands of direct suppliers that source everything from grains and nuts to vegetables and proteins. Plus, the company's supply chain is many layers deep—reaching all the way to the farmer growing crops or raising animals that will eventually reach the consumer as ConAgra products.

The complexity of the company's supply chain "forces us to prioritize and focus, balancing the relative climate impact and risk of an ingredient with our ability to influence change," explained Thompson.

Streamlining Supply Transport

That concern extends throughout the chain, even beyond the farm to the processing plants and transportation of products. ConAgra used to produce Hunt's tomato and pasta sauces in Newport, Tennessee and then ship the products nearly 3,000 miles to sell in Canada. It took 940 tandem trucks and 100 60-foot boxcars to transport the products. When the company decided to move production to Dresden, Ontario, it was able to streamline transportation by using just under 600 tri-axle trucks and 93 50-foot boxcars. The change reduced the route in Canada by 800 miles and shed 1.4 million miles from the company's network, cutting GHG emissions by 2,100 metric tons annually.

Social Supply

Adding to the supply chain sustainability puzzle is the frequent intersection of social and environmental issues throughout the chain, explained Thompson: "Take palm oil, for example. Southeast Asia is indisputably the most efficient growing area for palm plantations, contributing to the economic development of the region; but the area also has high natural capital value [that competes with demand for] greater transparency and pressures into supply chains for agriculture to continue to gain momentum and may change how we source ingredients longer term."

To ensure that its palm oil purchases don't add to deforestation of rainforests, further exacerbating climate change, the company pledged to source all of its palm oil from responsible and sustainable sources by December 2015.

If that move is any indication, ConAgra is poised to continue forging a sustainable path to climate resilience—ensuring availability of sources and food, while reducing GHG emissions.

Conclusion

Supply Chain Resilience

Improvements throughout the supply chain—from the farm, to the production line, and in transportation of food and supplies—is one way ConAgra is adapting to the shifts climate (including sudden events like floods or hurricanes and ongoing conditions like droughts), that directly affect farm productivity, which, in turn, affects the food supply. Such conditions can also affect food processing and transportation, as when electric utilities or critical modes of transportation (e.g., roads, rail) interrupt plant operations and transport of products.

Having been affected by Hurricane Sandy, the Missouri River floods, and drought conditions in the western US, ConAgra is especially cognizant of potential interruptions to its supply chain, and is taking measures to prepare by changing operations in anticipation of more to come. For instance, understanding that an especially long haul of tomato sauce—all the way from the southern US to Canada—might encounter climate interruptions, the company took steps to move the sauce production to Canada, slashing the mileage of the haul. Happy by-products include cutting both cost and GHGs from using less fuel for fewer, smaller vehicles traveling shorter distances.

Supply Endpoint: Waste Not, Profit More—from Cost to Opportunity

Because agriculture and food production generate so much waste—from farm to table and beyond—and a high proportion of GHG emissions,[10] one of ConAgra's top goals is to continue to slash waste throughout its facilities and its vast, complex supply chain, as demonstrated by its 2015 commitment to join other companies in halving waste by 2030.

---

[10] 24 percent of global GHG emissions in 2010. IPCC, (2014). Summary for Policymakers. In: *Climate Change 2014: Mitigation of Climate Change. Contribution of Working Group III to the Fifth Assessment Report of the Intergovernmental Panel on Climate Change* [Edenhofer, O., R. Pichs-Madruga, Y. Sokona, E. Farahani, S. Kadner, K. Seyboth, A. Adler, I. Baum, S. Brunner, P. Eickemeier, B. Kriemann, J. Savolainen, S. Schlömer, C. von Stechow, T. Zwickel and J.C. Minx (eds.)]. Cambridge, UK and New York, NY, USA: Cambridge University Press, 2014. p. 354.

Reducing waste not only helps cut GHGs and slash costs, it can also boost revenues. Both the dough and pudding examples illustrate the principle: by fixing a line at the dough facility to reduce overhang that was headed for a landfill, the company is now able to package and sell dough that was once waste. Likewise, an insight regarding mixed-flavor pudding, previously sent to landfill because it could not be sold, helped create a new market at correctional facilities for what was formerly waste—and boost revenue at the same time.

People in the Chain

One key to profiting from climate resilience through projects like waste reduction is to engage employees. Employee training and engagement in green efforts, both at the management and worker level, can lead to improvements in sustainability and profitability.

People want to help. Once aware and informed, employees and others, like suppliers—including, for ConAgra, farmers—are eager to jump on the bandwagon to do the right thing and contribute to the company's sustainability efforts. In this case, reducing GHGs and water waste was achieved by adopting cutting-edge technologies, limiting waste on the farm and in the production lines, and reducing energy use at the plant and on the road. Such changes help shave costs, boosting the bottom line while minimizing waste and GHGs.

What's more, once engaged, people's keen observations and ingenuity can help create opportunities, not only saving costs but also helping boosting profit from changes they initiate—as the dough and pudding examples show.

Additionally, vendors, like farmers and suppliers, are a key component of the final product and its impact. These suppliers, too, can willingly join the effort if provided with the right training and support.

Mitigation and Adaptation go Hand in Glove

ConAgra's actions demonstrate that climate mitigation—reducing GHGs at the source and throughout the supply and value chains—need not interfere with adapting to changing climate conditions. On the contrary, awareness feeds action and vice versa. To cut GHGs (via energy efficiency, smaller transportation fleets, waste reduction throughout the chain) and prepare for future interruptions, ConAgra created initiatives to improve sustainability in all aspects of its business. From limiting water used by suppliers (farmers) at the source, to limiting waste throughout processing and transport of products (i.e., diverting waste from landfill, often to productive processes), the company has shown that mitigation and adaptation efforts go hand in hand.

Part II: Decarbonizing the Supply Chain at Stonyfield Farm

As the planet warms, humans aren't the only ones feeling the heat. Even as we're advised that at extremely high temperatures humans can actually stop sweating,[11] it seems cows are already complaining viscerally.

No, they're not mooing more. They're just producing less milk. That's the bottom-line finding of a Department of Agriculture (DOA) study investigating climate change, heat stress, and dairy production. "Dairy cows are particularly sensitive to heat stress; higher temperatures lower milk output as well as its fat, solids, lactose, and protein content," the authors explain. In 2010 alone, heat stress accounted for a loss of $1.2 billion in production for the US dairy sector. And, as average temperatures rise from 1.45 to 2.37° F by 2030, the authors estimate the stress will decrease total milk production from 0.05 percent to 4.4 percent, with the greatest losses in southern US states.[12]

Raising Cows, Training Farmers

That's one reason Stonyfield Farm, headquartered in the northern state of New Hampshire, has been looking to nurture not just organic cows for its famed yogurt—but also the farmers, who are a vital part of the organic food company's supply chain. Stonyfield is now fully owned by the Paris-based multinational Danône, though its founder, Gary Hirshberg, who grounded the company in sustainability principles, still serves as chairman of its advisory board.

In order to ensure a continued healthy supply of organic milk from which to make its dairy products, in 2014 Stonyfield made an innovative decision to train organic dairy farmers. The move garnered a $1.5 million investment from parent company Danône, through its

---

[11]Manier, Jeremy, and Brendan McCarthy. (2016). "Athlete or Couch Potato, Heat Beats All." *The Chicago Tribune*. July 18, (2006). http://articles.chicagotribune.com/2006-07-18/news/0607180075_1_heat-wave-heat-cramps-heat-exhaustion

[12]Key, Nigel, Stacy Sneeringer, and David Marquardt. Climate Change, Heat Stress, and U.S. Dairy Production, ERR-175, U.S. Department of Agriculture, Economic Research Service. (September 2014). p. iii.

international Ecosystème Fund program that finances strategic partnerships, and an additional $150,000 investment from Stonyfield. The training farm, located at the nonprofit Wolfe's Neck in Freeport, Maine, raised additional funding for a total of $2 million, expected to finance the program for three years during its launch period. Subsequently, the farm expects the training program to be self-sustaining through dairy product sales, mainly to Stonyfield.

Packaging and Transporting Organic Milk

While Stonyfield's supply chain may not be as vast or complex as ConAgra's, the smaller, more specialized company sources packaging and other materials, in addition to its primary product, milk. The company transports its products, as well, a process that contributes to total GHG emissions from farm to spoon.[13]

Because Stonyfield is relatively small and specializes in dairy products (though it also makes soy yogurt), its supply chain is simpler and less extensive than a more diversified multinational food company. The dairy company primarily sources milk from the Wisconsin-based CROPP cooperative, which, in turn, sources the milk from farmers across the country and sells products under the Organic Valley brand name.

Stonyfield also monitors the sourcing of its packaging. In 2010, the company introduced plant-based packaging, a biodegradable thermoplastic aliphatic polyester made from renewable resources like corn starch that have less environmental impact than plastic. Additionally, Stonyfield works with like-minded suppliers in far-flung fields like finance and software.

Tracing Food Supply

The food industry has become so complex that it can be difficult to trace a product's source—mainly because products are moved so frequently. That's particularly true for grain, explained Erin Fitzgerald, Senior Vice President of the Innovation Center for US Dairy. While the dairy industry has a long history of cooperatives that aggregate milk, they have

---

[13]Some of the company's supply chain production and environmental footprint have been outlined in a 2001 life cycle study conducted by researchers at the University of Michigan.

Cutting GHGs from Farm to Table and Beyond: Players in the Supply Chain

Danône, Stonyfield Farm's parent company
- Provided financing for Stonyfield's organic dairy training farm
- Based on Stonyfield's experiment, began to use plant-based packaging

Wolfe's Neck Farm
- Partnership with Stonyfield to train organic dairy farmers
- Partnership with Department of Labor's accredited Dairy Grazing Apprenticeship program

Sourcemap
- Software company Stonyfield supported when it was a graduate student project
- Now helps the company track sourcing of its products and interface with suppliers and customers

Iroquois Farm
- First impact investor brought into Stonyfield's farmer training program
- Expects to help finance graduating farmers

Coulee Region Organic Produce Pool (CROPP)
- Dairy cooperative in Wisconsin, from which Stonyfield sources much of its organic milk supply

Asociación de Pequeños Productores de Talamanca (Association of Small Producers of Talamanca - APPTA)
- Association of small producers in Costa Rica from which Stonyfield sources bananas
- Building a processing plant, with support from Stonyfield and Sustainable Food Lab, to simplify the supply chain and return more control to farmers

Plant-based (Polylactic Acid or PLA) Packaging
- Stonyfield pioneered lighter, plant-based yogurt cups made of polylactic acid, in order to reduce the weight and emissions of product transport

- Through Working Landscapes Certificate program run by IATP in Nebraska, Stonyfield pays farmers to grow non-GMO corn, in order to compensate for the possible non-GMO corn in the unsegregated supply from which PLA material is made

Bio digester
- Stonyfield's manufacturing plant, takes in liquid waste from ingredients, releasing methane that captures and burns energy, while releasing treated wastewater directly to Londonberry's system

started to work directly with brands like Stonyfield to create a basic system of traceability for food safety reasons.

Dr. Leo Bonanni, CEO of Sourcemap, a software firm that allows companies to trace their supply chains by interacting with suppliers and sharing the information with customers, added that in the food sector "it's virtually impossible to know exactly where a product is sourced." Sourcemap, initially Bonanni's doctoral thesis project, was supported by Stonyfield, among others, while he was still conducting research as a student at MIT. Inspired by his work, the dairy company built Stonyfield's Sourcemap. Bonanni said a third of Sourcemap's work is with the food industry, due in part to the complexity of the supply chain in the food sector.

"What's more, because of its deeply cultural significance, where food comes from matters more to many people than what it is," he observed, adding that "issues of adulteration, safety, and health in the food industry [are among] topics that Americans—and people everywhere in the world—care about most."

Where Milk Comes From

The dairy business is so diversified that it's often difficult to trace the source of a particular product, even milk, partly because it's blended. "People think a single farm supplies one glass of milk, and it's not the case," said Fitzgerald. "You're mixing things, [but] the consumer wants to see one farm that makes the food, so that's the disconnect with traceability," throughout the chain, she explained. "[Supply] changes every day, and there might be 1,000 farms in the supplier network," further complicating attempts to trace the milk's source. What's more, 97 percent of dairy farms are family owned, and nearly 90 percent are affiliated with co-ops.

While Stonyfield currently works primarily with the CROPP cooperative based in Wisconsin to source milk, it does use other suppliers, including some smaller farms and processors. Hopes are that the nascent organic dairy training program will add newly trained organic farmers to the company's supply chain, as it also recruits existing organic farmers in New England.

Significantly, the company also uses other ingredients in its dairy products, including fruit, honey, chocolate, vanilla, and chia. In some cases, Stonyfield has direct relationships with the processors or the farms that grow those ingredients. For example, in Costa Rica where Stonyfield sources bananas, the company works with the cooperative APPTA. Again with a grant from parent company Danône's Ecosystème Fund, Stonyfield and the Sustainable Food Lab are working with APPTA to help it build its own processing plant,[14] which simplifies the supply chain by removing the middlemen and returning more control to the farmers.[15] Sourcemap has also helped Stonyfield learn more about its fruit suppliers in the United States.

A Changing Food Climate

Climate change is already affecting the agricultural and food supply chain (e.g., through droughts), and there are more impacts to come particularly for, according to reports (including the 2015 *Risky Business* report on the Midwest) the area considered the breadbasket of the United States.[16] Like

---

[14]Stonyfield in collaboration with Sustainable Food Lab launched the CAPE project aimed at designing an organic fruit processing unit for small- and medium-sized farms. This project is both intended to allow farmers to reduce their losses in the production and increase their income. Danône. 2014. Sustainability Report 2014.

[15]Stonyfield helped to support the development of a banana cooperative in Costa Rica, along with the development of the (Cellular Aseptic Processing Equipment) CAPE Project,16 an organic fruit-processing facility designed to help small- and medium-sized farms cut losses that stemmed from transporting produce to a processing plant at great distance.

[16]Gordon, Kate. (2015). *Risky Business: Economic Risks Of Climate Change In The United States.*

other *Risky Business* reports, this one was supported by a consortium of prominent financial experts, among others, including Michael Bloomberg and former US Secretaries of Treasury, Robert Rubin and Hank Paulson.

"Global warming [will affect] the availability of commodities like cocoa, sugar, avocados and so on, so [the issue] has come to light, and companies are trying to do what's possible," explained Sourcemap's Bonanni. "Usually that means engaging more with suppliers—especially farmers—to make sure that better practices are in place, and to work with farmers and others on improving their practices."

Training Farmers

Stonyfield stays abreast of climate change and other trends that can affect its milk supply. Those could include factors such as the general waning of dairy farming in the Northeast: In 1965, Vermont had 6,000 dairies, compared with under 1,000 in 2015, while in 2000, Maine had 500 dairy farms, versus 300. The company points out that milk production in the region overall hasn't yet declined, since more cows per farm are producing more milk per cow.

However, the cost of caring for cows and producing organic milk has gone up over time, according to Stonyfield. The biggest cost to dairy farmers is feed; higher feed prices recently have increased the cost of production. One way to roughly estimate the increase in costs, Stonyfield explained, is by the price of organic milk, which from 2000 to 2015, had almost doubled from around $19 per hundred pounds of milk to about $37.

As risks to supply continue, Stonyfield needs to ensure it can offer the products its customers want from trusted sources. That led the company to partner on its farmer training program with the nonprofit Wolfe's Neck. Part of the training program entails providing pathways for trainees to eventually own farms, which in turn means learning about lenders. Those include traditional lenders like the Farm Service Agency, a part of the U.S. Department of Agriculture. Stonyfield is also introducing trainees to so-called impact investment firms, which, the company believes, would find sustainable agriculture to be a good investment opportunity. The first investor brought to the program was Iroquois Valley, an Evanston, Illinois private equity firm focused on organic farming. The first organic dairy trainees graduating from Wolfe's Neck in mid-2017 will have had exposure to such investors.

At its core, Stonyfield's training program, launched in mid-2015, is one way for the dairy company to ensure it gets a steady supply of organic milk from local family farms by training the next generation of organic dairy farmers—all while keeping GHG emissions low on the farms and on the haul (which, from local farms, will be closer to Stonyfield's main facility in Londonderry, New Hampshire than ever before).

Exactly how those goals are accomplished—and how much the program can drive down GHG emissions—remains to be seen, explained Liza Dube, Stonyfield's Director of PR and Digital Marketing:

> We won't have an actual idea of the differences until we can get farmers to work with a regimen of what they'll be learning through a more holistic approach to figuring out how to be an organic dairy farmer through sustainable farming and sustainable business tied together as a single system. Stonyfield will be learning along the way. That's the nature of organic, because we're always discovering new ways of doing things. There's an idea that organic is the old-fashioned way, but it's way more advanced than people could imagine.

Explained Britt Lundgren, Stonyfield's Director of Organic and Sustainable Agriculture, about the training:

> This is still a very small, slow launch, because we want to focus on the close proximity of farms near our plant—that is, in northern New England and parts of New York State, to reduce emissions from hauling the milk. We partnered with Wolfe's Neck Farm in Maine because their farmland is dedicated to conservation, and they were trying to understand what they could do for sustainable agriculture in Maine and the Northeastern US. Lots of young people are interested in going into sustainable agriculture, but it can be expensive and they don't necessarily have much equity saved, so we do see growth in new farmers—but not in organic dairy farmers.

Hence, the company's interest in offering exposure to financial help from like-minded investors like Iroquois. She added:

We talked with Wolfe's Neck about this problem and got excited about training students—four at a time over a two-year residential program, where they live on site at the farm in Freeport and learn organic dairy farming management, pasture management, animal health, business planning. They're not learning how to milk a cow.

The program partners with Dairy Grazing Apprenticeship, accredited through the US Department of Labor. As part of the graduation requirement, students will present a business plan "to real, live investors," Lundgren noted. "That's the key thing that's new about this program—it's the only one focused on organizational farm management."

Down on the Farm

Wolfe's Neck was thinking along complementary lines. A nonprofit working and demonstration farm cum educational center, with 626 acres in Freeport, Maine along four miles of ocean coastline, Wolfe's Neck organizes activities to connect people of all ages to sustainable agriculture, farming and their sources of food. "About three years ago, we launched a strategic process with the intent and hope of finding a new and meaningful program and project to launch as part of growing and strengthening food systems in this area," explained Executive Director David Herring. "We had become aware of New England Food Vision, a 50-year look at how we can create a stronger food system for the Northeast to provide more food for ourselves instead of [relying on] outside regions. Now roughly 10 percent of the food we consume is grown here. One goal outlined in Food Vision is to be at 50 percent by 2060," he said.

Achieving that goal will require significant shifts such as "changing our eating habits and leveraging the strength and assets we have in the Northeast, including things like climate, soils, existing infrastructure and heritage," he added. Herring continued:

We produce a lot less food for ourselves than we used to, and there used to be many more family-run, smaller farms in the Northeast and Maine. Then the growth of big, industrial agriculture over the past several decades led to a decline in smaller farms that the Northeast is well set up for. The big monoculture farm, mainly in the Midwest and focused mainly on one crop, isn't what the Northeast is set up for. We don't have the vast expanse of land that's appropriate for that. We wanted to play a meaningful role in supporting the vision of small-scale farms that work here.

Historically we've been a livestock farm raising beef cattle, with several hundred acres of pasture. But our goal isn't just to raise animals to eat them. We wanted to find a higher calling to use our resources and assets and decided on training new livestock farmers, especially those focused on pasture-based farming. It was during that period when we were introduced to the folks at Stony-field and began to learn more about the organic dairy business and the challenges and opportunities that currently exist.

One of the opportunities, especially for Maine, is for there to be more production, more farms, cows and milk. That would be a great thing for Maine. It would help support rural economies, create jobs, and benefit the environment. Instead of shipping in conventional milk, we can produce organic milk. Stonyfield is looking for more organic milk, and demand is rising. So what we're going to do is train the next generation of organic dairy farmers. And one thing we know is that we have a climate in Maine that's conducive to dairy farming, so we feel that, even with climate change, we'll be well-positioned for dairy production.

Potentially, organic dairy farming could help reduce GHGs, according to a 2011 USDA report called *Putting Dairy Cows to Pasture: And Environmental Plus.* One study detailed in the report found that dairy cows on pasture produce 8 percent less GHGs than cows kept in confinement.[17]

Fitzgerald noted that organic dairy farming includes just two requirements – that cows remain on pasture for 120 days and that any pesticides used be organic. This definition, however, doesn't include GHG emissions levels, water use, or quality and efficiency of farming practices.

In its first class, trainees in the Stonyfield program have already honed some skills at organic dairies or in degree programs—including how

---

[17]Perry, Ann, "Putting Dairy Cows to Pasture: An Environmental Plus," *Agricultural Research.* (2011). 19.

to operate equipment, how to locate and milk animals, how to put up hay. The program began with 30 cows, with expected growth to 60 by mid-2016.

"We'll focus on helping [trainees] create plans to transition onto a farm and start their own operations," Herring explained. That transition planning will start at the beginning of the program, focusing on business skills, financial management, stockmanship, animal handling, health management and nutrition, growing and harvesting feed, grazing management, and dairy operations.

Trainees will eventually present a business plan to investors, so helping them find money is part of the transition planning process. Iroquois Valley was the first impact investor brought in to assist with the financing process. As a private equity company, it connects investors with organic farmland. The firm, founded in 2007 as the first of its kind in the United States, currently owns 28 farms in seven states, totaling over 3,600 acres of land that is organic or in transition to organic. Over $16 million of the farmland is leased through the firm's Young Farmer Land Access Program. Through that program, the firm extends minimum five-year leases to its farmers, requiring them to transition land to organic-certified status. In its B Corp statement, the firm writes: "The Company goal is to have multi-generational impact, keeping the farmer on the land." Such goals are in line with Stonyfield's organic farmer training program.

Cutting Emissions: Cows, Plastics, and Hauls

Stonyfield is continually on the lookout for ways to reduce GHGs during production and throughout its supply chain, packaging, and transport. Indeed, the company has been an early influence for Danône in setting worldwide goals for sustainable agriculture.

Stonyfield piloted plant-based (PLA) "plastic" materials for yogurt containers and was among the first to do a life cycle analysis for its products, pioneering GHG tracking "from farm emissions to keeping yogurt in the fridge—from farm to spoon," said Lundgren. Over half (roughly 52 percent) of Stonyfield's emissions come from agriculture (mostly from milk, by far its biggest ingredient).

Manure also releases emissions. Explained Lundgren:

Different ways of storing manure have different levels of emissions and different types of GHGs. If manure is stored as a liquid, then it's released as methane; if it's stored as a solid and dry-stacked, then it's more nitrogen emissions. There's an emerging body of research on this, but Stonyfield was one of the first companies trying to understand where the emissions were coming from and what to do about it.

"Then there are the emissions from the cows themselves," Lundgren continued:

The enteric fermentation—burping and farting—releases methane, an incredibly potent GHG. So we've been thinking for a long time about how to get better at reducing emissions on the farm and work with farmers to help them reduce emissions in ways that don't add to the farmers' costs.

One of the biggest challenges is that it's not as simple as if you store manure this way or feed cows that, you'll [save] X amount of methane. For instance, in 2009, we did a "Greener Cow" Pilot. [The pilot] predicted that if you feed flax seeds to cows, it will reduce emissions from enteric fermentation and increase omega free fatty acids in milk, which are very beneficial.

So we had nine or 10 farms in a pilot feeding flax seed to cows and modeled the GHG reductions and found we were successful in reducing emissions and increasing omega. We got really excited and wanted all our farmers to do it, but before going forward, we needed to do more to validate the methodology behind the model. We brought in some academics to help us. They did a trial very similar to what we'd done, but this trial tracked the reality, and it became clear [our] model wasn't accurate.

More research needs to be done on this, and we're continuing to explore alternatives and evaluate tools on how to measure emissions on the farm accurately, so the farmers can [take meaningful steps] on the farm to help reduce emissions. There's no simple solution.

Of Cups and Corn

"We're always looking at how we can reduce emissions from shipping our products to the grocery store by improving logistics or using rail instead of trucking or lightening the plastic for non-PLA cups to reduce the weight of the load," Lundgren said.

Other steps to reduce Stonyfield's GHG emissions affect packaging, manufacturing, transportation, and energy efficiency, as they investigate "all points on the chain for opportunities to reduce GHGs, from manufacturing facilities to reducing energy [consumption] and using renewable energy," she added. "We have a bio-digester on our site in Londonderry, where we have most of our manufacturing. The bio-digester acts like a giant stomach: it takes in liquid waste from our plant, yogurt and whey, and the bacteria in it digest nutrients and release methane in a way that [we can] capture and burn [for] energy. The wastewater that comes out is effectively treated and can go directly into the town's system without hurting it and burdening the town."

The company has switched from petroleum-based plastic to plant-based materials for packaging its products wherever possible. "We've pioneered the use of PLA, polylactic acid, made from corn, which is a renewable resource, and drastically lowers GHGs associated with packaging," explained Lundgren. However, the company can use this packaging only for some four-ounce cups, mainly because the material isn't strong enough to be molded into a single-serve cup or other products, she said.

The PLA material "arrives to us as a rolled up flat sheet," Lundgren explained. "At our facility, the sheet goes into a machine that pushes it into shape, and another area of the machine gets it filled with yogurt. A third part of the machine gets it sealed with a lid." Lundgren added that this is an adaptation of a commonly used machine that typically processes petroleum-based materials.

Stonyfield Farm products are certified organic, which prohibits GMOs. When the company launched its plant-based packaging, there wasn't a big enough segregated supply of non-GMO corn from which to produce the PLA they needed. Nonetheless, Stonyfield offsets possible GMOs in the PLA-based material by working through the Institute for Agriculture and Trade Policy (IATP). The Institute then works with a group of farmers (mainly in Nebraska), and pays them a premium to grow non-GMO corn.

Explained Lundgren about the process: "Since we couldn't guarantee [the corn] wasn't GMO, we partnered with some farmers to pay them to grow non-GMO corn, so that for every acre of corn that goes into the cup, we're paying the farmer to grow an acre of non-GMO [corn]," through the Working Landscapes Certificate program run by the IATP.

Because it's lighter and reduces the overall load weight, the PLA material, despite its limited application, has helped reduce emissions from shipping the product to grocery stores. Stonyfield has made an effort to improve logistics, too, using rail instead of trucking when possible. Another win: Stonyfield's example allowed parent Danône to begin using PLA in its yogurt product line.

Conclusion

As the climate changes, cows have already begun producing less milk. For a dairy producer, like Stonyfield, this is a monumental risk. To manage the risk, the company works to abate it—by reducing GHGs from farm to table and beyond—and to adapt innovatively throughout its supply chain. Stonyfield, whose core product is organic and whose sustainability mission drives its reputation, is constantly seeking ways to ensure that its entire supply chain – from financing and training new organic farmers to integrating a software approach of tracking product to the materials used in packaging – is aligned with these values.

Supply Chain Resilience

Stonyfield's nascent organic farmer training program offers innovative lessons to other industries. As it faces the reality of climate change, Stonyfield is tackling the potential scarcity of its core product—organically produced milk—through multiple creative means. To ensure its supply, while cutting GHGs along the chain, Stonyfield is training organic dairy farmers throughout New England and in northern New York, near its main facility in New Hampshire. This will add additional milk supply to the company's main source—a dairy co-op in Wisconsin—by ensuring there are more organic dairy farms run by trained organic farmers. What's more, by ensuring that the farms are near its main production facility, the company lowers GHG emissions by reducing the length of the haul.

The training program also helps a nonprofit farm in Maine, with which Stonyfield is partnering, by offering it the opportunity to expand from beef production to something it considers to be a higher, more sustainable calling: producing more locally grown, organic products, training a new generation of farmers, and boosting the regional economy.

Getting to Know the Supplier

Know your supplier as well as your customer. That might well be Stonyfield's motto, as it confronts the changing climate.

Stonyfield has shown that learning about the source of products—as well as the end user—is now more possible, thanks to new technologies. Importantly, the company's supply chain resilience is supported by Sourcemap. This innovative software offers Stonyfield a way to dig deep into its chain to learn more about its suppliers, while allowing its customers to learn more about where their food comes from.

To accomplish its current goal of training organic dairy farmers who may one day become suppliers themselves, Stonyfield again shows that a little ingenuity may also help create financial sourcing opportunities with like-minded investors such as Iroquois Valley, whose mission is to help young organic farmers through its financing program.

The company's "get-to-know-your-supplier" approach isn't just for more abstract supplies like technology and finance. It's applied to bananas, too. While a source that's secondary to milk for Stonyfield, bananas are an example of how getting to know the supplier can lead to sustainable sourcing over the long run. Supporting the suppliers—banana farmers—will help ensure that the fruit is available to Stonyfield in perpetuity.

Adapting While Mitigating

Stonyfield doesn't stop at innovating for climate adaptation. The company continues to look for ways to lower GHG emissions throughout its production cycle, starting at the farm and moving beyond, by reducing the weight of its packaging or switching to renewably sourced, plant-based packaging, lightening and shortening the haul of supplies transported to and from its facility, and recycling waste into energy at its facility.

In ensuring that its organic, low-GHG supply chain is in line with its sustainability values, the company's rigor and leadership is striking: from connecting with suppliers and customers on social media, to training organic dairy farmers, to discovering ways to reduce GHGs on the farm, to shortening and lightening the haul of goods, to using renewable packaging, to recycling the waste, to partnering with a mission-based firm to help finance trainees in its organic farmer training effort.

CHAPTER 4

Taking a Risk—and Managing It

Insuring Climate Risk: The Hartford

European reinsurers like Swiss Re and Munich Re have been advocating for attention to climate change for decades. Of course, the industry has an almost desperate stake in urging intelligent response to the changing climate: as insurers of last resort—insurers to the insurance companies—reinsurers are left holding the bag and paying the piper when climate disasters hit.

But insurers themselves are just one step removed from the front lines of the reinsurance industry—and closer to the businesses and individuals they insure. So it's sad to see that, with so many opportunities to raise awareness about climate—and even potentially to profit from that—the US insurance industry has lagged.

A 200-year-old-plus U.S. insurer may change that trend. Eyeing opportunity in risk and risk management—arguably the insurance sector's specialty—The Hartford, a nearly $20 billion property and casualty company, has been taking a low-carbon future seriously since 2007 by decreasing its own greenhouse gas (GHG) emissions in facilities, empowering its employees with alternative ways of commuting, insuring the renewable energy industry, and perhaps most important, offering new insurance products to incentivize businesses and individuals alike to cut greenhouse gas emissions and reduce climate risk exposure.

The Hartford was one of only two insurers headquartered in the United States to earn a "Leading" rating—among 330 companies queried—in a fall 2014 report issued by the Coalition of Environmentally Responsible

Economies (CERES), a nonprofit organization that for decades has been urging companies, investors, and others to change their approach to climate. That's especially noteworthy, given that only nine insurers achieved the high rating.

Called *Insurer Climate Risk Disclosure Survey Report & Scorecard: 2014 Findings & Recommendations*,[1] the report ranks insurers representing some 87 percent of the US market—in the property and casualty, life and annuities, and health insurance sectors. Based on 2013 disclosures to a climate risk survey developed by the National Association of Insurance Commissioners (NAIC), the report ranks the companies on climate indicators, including governance, risk and investment strategies, GHG management, and public engagement (e.g., climate policy). Even after Hurricane Sandy caused losses of over $75 billion,[2] US insurers have remained largely "risk-averse" when it comes to promoting climate precautions, even as they become increasingly vulnerable to the financial risks of more frequent and intense weather events that boost damages and losses across the country.

Risk-Reward Quotient

But as The Hartford's approach shows, risk aversion can also lead to opportunity. Launched in 2007 (thanks to the urging of the insurer's then-general counsel, who championed the initiative after it was brought to his attention by an investor group), the firm's low-carbon commitment includes reporting to the CDP (previously the Carbon Disclosure Project) issuing a climate change action statement, and creating an environmental committee that oversees climate change strategy—all as part of its overall sustainability initiative.

Today, the company's general counsel and executive vice president, Alan Kreczko, chairs the 15-person environment committee, with leaders

---

[1]CERES. (2014). "Insurer Climate Risk Disclosure Survey Report & Scorecard: 2014 Findings & Recommendations." Accessed January 4, 2016. https://www.ceres.org/resources/reports/insurer-climate-risk-disclosure-survey-report-scorecard-2014-findings-recommendations/view.

[2]Huang, Chongfu, Abdelouahid Lyhyaoui, and Zhai Guofang, Nesrin Benhayoun. Emerging Economies, Risk and Development, and Intelligent Technology In: *Proceedings of the 5th International Conference on Risk Analysis and Crisis Response*. CRC Press, Oxford, May 26, 2015.

from company functions ranging from risk management to service operations, consumer markets, sales, and investing and government affairs. In 2011, the firm added volunteers from its early-career professional program to join the environment committee, assigning them to engage employees on environmental stewardship; those volunteers launched a subcommittee that meets monthly.

By 2010, the firm had launched its renewable energy practice to insure the renewable energy sector—wind, solar, and fuel cell companies. Three years later, in 2013 the insurer earned over $4 million in earned premiums (or pro-rated premiums paid in advance that are now the insurer's) from that business, up from $1.2 million in 2011.

"We talk about how, as the economy changes—for example as we're seeing more renewable energy projects—we see an opportunity for insurance," said Jay Bruns, the company's Environmental Champion, noting that the The Hartford identified insurance gaps that didn't exist with traditional energy production. Risks insuring fossil fuel energy projects are typically about whether, for instance, there will be a stable supply of natural gas. The different risks for renewables imply different insurance needs, and such risks can spell opportunity for an insurer. The Hartford was one of the first companies to offer such insurance in the United States.

The insurance for renewables covers a variety of risks, such as intermittency: If, for instance, the wind doesn't blow or the sun doesn't shine, then insurance might cover the peril for the company that can't provide the energy it promised. The Hartford also offers "end-to-end" coverage for companies in the renewable energy business—from R&D, to delivery of power and performance once they're operating. The firm also offers general liability and workers' compensation insurance, for the different risks of renewable energy facilities, including construction of wind and solar farms.

Much of what owners and operators of renewable energy projects want can be provided by the insurer, and a great deal of what they need overlaps with what traditional energy producers need. There's inherent risk in running a power plant—whether the power is generated by a wind turbine or natural gas. But some risks are different, such as how workers might be hurt and what sorts of injuries they sustain.

The Harford sees its renewable energy business mainly as a growth opportunity, earning over $6 million in earned premiums from its renewable energy practice in 2014, up from $4 million in 2013 and $3 million in 2012. In its 2015 CDP submission, the company adds that with renewable energy investment in the United States of $41 billion for the year, "the upside in future years could be considerable." In its sustainability report for 2013, the company adds that it underwrites 15 fuel cell generation plants, increasing capacity to take on larger exposure in renewable plants. "With 90 wind farms currently under construction in 20 U.S. states, we are expecting to grow this book of business significantly over the next five years." (Further analysis of the Hartford's other climate products and services is below, in the section titled "From the inside out.")

General counsel Alan Kreczko explained: "We believe that understanding the risks associated with climate change, coupled with environmentally responsible business practices, will enhance The Hartford's competitive position, but as importantly, they are simply the right things to do."[3]

Risk of Changing Rules for a Changing Climate

Understanding climate risks could prove to be the "right" thing to do in more ways than one. The insurance industry is regulated in the United States on a state-by-state basis, and, increasingly, state regulators are asking insurers to disclose their climate risks and responsibilities.

As of 2013, eight states—California, Connecticut, Illinois, Minnesota, New York, Washington, New Mexico, and Maryland—require insurance companies that sell above a certain amount of insurance to report on climate risks.[4] In 2013, insurance commissioners "required insurers writing more than $100 million in direct [coverage] to disclose their climate-related risks," according to the CERES report.

---

[3]CERES. (2014). "First-of-its-Kind Report Ranks U.S. Insurance Companies on Climate Change Responses." Accessed January 4, 2016. http://www.ceres.org/press/press-releases/first-of-its-kind-report-ranks-u.s.-insurance-companies-on-climate-change-responses.
[4]"Climate Risk Disclosure Survey". (2016). Insurance.Ca.Gov. http://www.insurance.ca.gov/0250-insurers/0300-insurers/0100-applications/ClimateSurvey/. Hirji, Zahra. 2014. "U.S. Insurers Meet Climate Risk With 'Deeply Troubling' Silence". *Inside Climate News*, (October 24, 2014)., Accessed June 11, 2016. http://insideclimatenews.org/news/20141023/us-insurers-meet-climate-risk-deeply-troubling-silence.

What's more, in his forward to the report, Washington Insurance Commissioner Mike Kreidler, also chair of NAIC's Climate Change and Global Warming Working Group, notes that it's high time insurers heeded signals and started leading the way on dampening risks. Explained Kreidler:

> With climate change, 97 percent of scientists in the field agree that it is a reality and are more focused on the timing and magnitude of changes and related damage we can expect. This industry should be focused less on what is causing climate change and more on how we respond to and mitigate it.
>
> As key regulators of this sector, we strongly encourage insurance industry leaders and investors who own these companies to take this challenge far more seriously. There is no doubt that an early effort to adjust policies, premiums, and insurance investments will result in less dramatic impacts later on, thus avoiding or reducing losses that we can already anticipate. The insurance industry, by being responsible and forward-looking, can lead the way to better public and private investments as well as more robust research and policy engagement to identify, quantify, and mitigate the key climate risks we all face. As this valuable report points out, the result will be an insurance industry whose markets expand rather than contract in the face of growing climate change risks.

As an example of mounting climate change awareness and activity in the insurance sector—and in an interesting twist on insurers' climate concerns—in May 2014, Farmers Insurance brought a lawsuit against nearly 200 Chicago-area communities alleging they didn't adequately act to prevent flooding in 2013. Rescinded less than two months later, the insurer's class-action suit sought reimbursement from local governments for claims it paid to over 600 property owners.[5] The unprecedented lawsuit was a wake-up call for municipalities and property owners alike, and

---

[5]McCoppin, Robert, Black, Lisa, and Dan Hinkel. (2014). "Insurers Sue Chicago-area Towns over Flood Money." *Chicago Tribune,* May 14, 2014, Accessed July 21, 2015. http://articles.chicagotribune.com/2014-05-14/news/ct-insurance-claims-flooding-met-20140514_1_flood-money-flood-zones-sewers.

the incident underscores that an increasingly volatile climate can, in turn, induce volatile business relationships.

Opportunity in Innovation: Kudos for Cuts

By contrast, The Hartford's climate approach, including its suite of products to encourage customers—both institutions and individuals—to reduce GHGs and increase resilience activities (to prepare for, withstand, and rebuild sensibly after extreme weather and other shocks) demonstrates that innovative business models can produce positive results for companies, customers, and other stakeholders. Importantly, in its 2014 report to the CDP, The Hartford also noted a number of potential regulatory changes related to climate that it follows closely as part of its risk management activities, underscoring the likelihood of increased regulatory attention to climate and acknowledging regulatory change as another potential risk to the company moving forward.

A top rating in the CERES report is hardly the first time The Hartford has been recognized for its forward-thinking climate policy and activities. The CERES ranking follows a consistent track record of recognition for the insurer's climate action. In 2014, The Hartford was again recognized for its climate activities by the Dow Jones Sustainability Index (DJSI) for a third year and by CDP's Leader Index for a seventh year. Both indices serve as benchmarks for investors who integrate sustainability into their portfolios. Also in 2014, the US Environmental Protection Agency (EPA) recognized The Hartford with an award for Excellence in Greenhouse Gas Management. Among the company's climate achievements: a net GHG emissions reduction of 42 percent from 2007 through 2012.

The Hartford also has an emerging climate resilience approach for itself, its assets, and employees, as outlined below in the section entitled "Internal Resilience and Enterprise Risk Management (ERM): Business Continuity and Risk Management for Catastrophe, Operations, Finance."[6]

---

[6]The Hartford. (2013). "The Hartford's Sustainability Report 2013." Accessed January 4, 2016. http://www.thehartford.com/sites/thehartford/files/sustainability-report-2013.pdf.

The company's approach to growing signs of climate change follows its longtime work in this area. Like other companies that have excelled in the environmental and sustainability arenas, The Hartford is proactive on resilience in the face of increasingly intense events including, in the United States alone, more frequent, intense hurricanes and ongoing droughts. The company has issued a sustainability report since 2009. The insurer has reported its GHG emissions to CDP since 2007 and from 2008 through 2014 has been on its Leadership Index. The company later reported retroactively from 2004.

In 2014, the insurer updated its climate policy after 7 years. The Harford also ensures that its electronics don't go to landfill and pursues a paper reduction effort.

Climate Resilience Opportunities

While The Hartford has consistently monitored and decreased its GHG emissions well down the supply chain—detailing its direct Scope 1,[7] indirect Scope 2 and indirect value chain Scope 3 emissions in its CDP report. Perhaps more notably, the company has also recognized and created business opportunities in the face of a changing climate, even as it adjusts its own resilience practices.

Some development of new products and services is a response to extreme weather events, which the company views as a "key risk."[8] In response, The Hartford "continually improves its techniques for managing these weather risks across the company and applies these tools on an enterprise basis. The critical importance of these robust processes has been highlighted by growing insured losses owing to severe weather events."

Such events potentially affect the insurer's customers—and therefore its investment holdings and risk exposure, since insurers reinvest the premiums they earn from customers into their own portfolios, mostly as treasuries and state municipal bonds that are generally considered to be relatively safe choices.

---

[7]See chapter 2 footnote 4.

[8]Carbon Disclosure Report. (2011). CDP 2011 Investor CDP 2011 Information Request. http://www.thehartford.com/higfiles/pdf/CDP,0.pdf.

The company has, since Hurricane Sandy, expanded products and services that respond to customers' changing needs and desires. In 2012, the year Hurricane Sandy struck, The Hartford paid out $706 million in weather-related catastrophe loss claims, down from $745 million the year before. In 2013, the company paid out $312 million in natural catastrophe claims "primarily due to multiple thunderstorm, hail and tornado events," according to its CDP report.

Small Business: From Response to Resilience

Also in response to Sandy, The Hartford reported the effects of the storm on over 450 small businesses in New York, New Jersey, and Connecticut, to gather information that could help small business owners in the future. "We looked at small companies that faced problems in the impact area and what they might do to protect themselves in the future," Bruns explained.

Highlights of the report, captured in an infographic entitled *The Hartford Small Business Pulse 2013: Storm Sandy*, note that 71 percent of small businesses experienced a power outage during the storm, while 52 percent lost revenue. Other top challenges included customer, employee, and supplier issues. Suggestions from small businesses that weathered the storm include such resilience measures as reviewing the business's property insurance policy, investing in a generator, creating a backup of records, and developing a business continuity plan. Explained Bruns:

> This is a key market for The Hartford, and we wanted to learn ourselves about the issues they face. One key take-away: a lot of people didn't back up their computers outside of their locations. Many are small Mom and Pop stores and they don't think through all the implications that large companies do, because the latter have more resources to devote to business resiliency.

The Hartford now hosts a website for small businesses where additional information about resiliency measures is available.

Beyond Catastrophes: Incentivizing Customers

At the most basic level, The Hartford helps customers affected by catastrophes bolster their own resilience. For weather-related and other emergencies, the company runs an emergency response center near Chicago, whose employees can "respond 24/7 to catastrophes," said Bruns. The center now has a fleet of emergency vans to help its customers, including an RV with satellite technology and enough power to support phone chargers, an ATM machine, televisions, and cooking facilities in areas that have lost power during tornadoes, hurricanes, earthquakes, and fires—where there are likely to be large, complex losses. Claims adjusters travel with the vans so that customers can file claims for losses in a timely fashion and move through the process efficiently.

Incentivizing its customers to adopt resiliency measures goes well beyond helping them through catastrophes once they've occurred. The Hartford had been promoting greater climate awareness and lower GHG emissions among its customers even before Hurricane Sandy galvanized US companies to begin tackling climate change and address resilience head on. The insurer now boasts a growing list of 11 such resilience products for its customers. For instance, since the 2010 launch of its Renewable Energy Practice insuring the wind, solar, and fuel cell industries described above, The Hartford's unit has "won the bid to insure the largest private solar panel installation in the Western Hemisphere, and now underwrites the only fuel cell plant operating in the world," according to its CDP report. What's more, "in a sign that the opportunities are growing"[9] since 2009, the company has been introducing products to help customers cut GHG emissions and generally reduce environmental impacts, including a discount for electric vehicle (EV) owners and clarification that homeowner policies cover EV charging stations in policyholders' garages.

From the Inside Out: Practice First, Preach Second

The introduction of these products for the company's customers partly grew out of The Hartford's own experience with electric cars. The insurer, already offering discounts for hybrid vehicles to its customers, invested in a charging company that offered to install EV charging stations at three

---

[9]CDP. (2012). "CDP (2012) Investor CDP 2012 Information Request: The Hartford Financial Services Group, Inc." Accessed January 4, 2015. http://www.thehartford.com/higfiles/pdf/CDP2012.pdf.

of The Hartford's premises. Despite the fact that the charging stations were donated, at each location The Hartford had to rip up the parking lot asphalt and cover the expensive installation costs. In 2011, the insurer's employees were able to plug in their cars and charge them for free, contributing to cuts in the the company's Scope 3 emissions. (Scope 3 emissions were further reduced as employees opted to embrace expanded opportunities to work from home.)

With a renewed dedication to EVs, the insurer began to offer a 5 percent premium discount for customers with EVs and hybrids, a first for a U.S. company. For commercial fleet policies, the Hartford offers a related product that offers additional coverage for hybrid vehicle upgrades; if a non-hybrid car in the fleet suffers a total loss, The Hartford pays up to $2,500 per car and $10,000 per policy when it's replaced with a hybrid. These products offer customers a way to reduce their own GHG output, while driving the same number of miles.

Similarly, if a homeowner or company's building suffers a loss, The Hartford offers incentives to rebuild to a higher environmental standard such as LEED certification or including features like bamboo flooring that can be agreed upon in advance, as described in the company's website:

- Green Homeowners Coverage (Personal homeowners— optional policy that expands coverage limits by up to 10 percent when an insured uses environmentally friendly materials or processes to make repairs or upgrades after a covered loss)
- Green Choice Additional Coverage (Commercial property— includes $100,000 coverage to upgrade to green alternatives in the event of a loss; can be applied to uses such as repair or replacement using more environmentally friendly materials, equipment, or processes, certification fees associated with LEED and other standards, or indoor air quality restoration or debris recycling systems)

The Hartford divides its 11 products designed to cut customers' GHG emissions in three main categories in its 2013 sustainability report.[10] These

---

[10]CDP. (2015). "CDP 2015 Climate Change 2015 Information Request: The Hartford Financial Services Group, Inc." Accessed January 4, 2016. http://www.thehartford .com/sites/thehartford/files/2015-CDP-projectsubmission.pdf.

products encourage customers to purchase hybrids or EVs through pre-mium discounts, expanding coverage to insured losses that "facilitate in-stallation of more energy efficient equipment and use of environmentally friendly materials," and options to reduce customer mailings.[11]

Summary of The Hartford's Sustainable Insurance Policies

Products for hybrids and EVs include:

- Hybrid Vehicle Credits (Personal Auto—5% credit to policies covering hybrid vehicles)
- Hybrid Vehicle Upgrade Coverage (Commercial Auto—if damage to a non-hybrid auto results in a total loss and is replaced with a hybrid, The Hartford pays an additional 10% of actual cash value up to $2500 per vehicle and $10,000 per policy)
- Electric Vehicle credits (Personal Auto—5% credit to policies covering EVs)

. . . The following products also allow policyholders to avoid GHG emissions:

- Green Homeowners Coverage (Personal Homeowners—optional coverage that expands coverage limits by up to 10% when an insured uses environmentally friendly materials or processes to make repairs or upgrades after a covered loss)
- Green Equipment Breakdown Coverage (Personal Homeowners—optional coverage that allows customers to replace broken down systems such as heating and cooling systems or refrigerators with more efficient systems that have achieved environmental certification)
- Electric Vehicle Chargers (Personal Homeowners—new policies clearly include home-based EV chargers as covered

(continued)

---

[11] The Hartford's Sustainability Report. (2013). The Hartford. Accessed January 4, 2016. http://www.thehartford.com/sites/thehartford/ "les/sustainability-re- port-2013.pdf.

property—"auto equipment" is typically excluded from
homeowners' policies)

- Green Choice Additional Coverage (Commercial Property—
  includes $100,000 coverage to upgrade to green alternatives
  in the event of a loss, can be applied to uses such as repair
  or replacement using environmentally friendly materials,
  equipment, or processes, certification fees associated with
  LEED and other standards, and indoor air quality restoration
  or debris recycling systems)
- Renewable Energy Equipment Choice (Commercial Marine—
  covers loss to renewable energy equipment including solar,
  wind, and geothermal)
- Green Builders Risk Endorsement (Commercial Marine—
  includes coverage on all Builder's Risk policies for building
  commissioning expense, certification fees, vegetative roofing,
  $50,000 debris recycling, and $50,000 indoor air quality testing)
- Equipment Breakdown Coverage Extension (Commercial
  Business Owners—as part of overall Special Property Coverage
  Form, the Hartford will pay up to additional 25% of cost to
  replace broken equipment with alternatives that are better for
  the environment, safer, or more efficient)

. . .We also offer a GHG-saving service to our customers under The
Hartford's paper suppression efforts:

- The Hartford plants a tree each time a customer switches
  from paper to eBilling, electronic funds transfer, or electronic-
  only delivery of their statements. 42,700 recipients of The
  Hartford mailings opted for e-delivery and that many trees
  were planted on their behalf. The paper suppression program is
  a component of the overall strategy. By allowing customers to
  opt into electronic delivery of their documents, the Hartford is
  projected to save more than $38 million in paper and postage
  over 5 years of the program.

Source: The Hartford's Sustainability Report. (2013). The Hartford. Accessed January 4,
2016. http://www.thehartford.com/sites/thehartford/ "les/sustainability-re- port-2013.pdf."

Market Needs and Opportunities

Much of The Hartford's proactive development of products and services to mitigate GHGs and build a cleaner climate comes from a simple response to market opportunities. "Generally, our industry follows all the industries," explained Bruns. "Their issues become our issues."

With floods or crop losses, the federal government holds the risk. But an insurer has to think through potential scenarios for other losses due to weather and price for them. The Hartford also offers workers' compensation insurance, so it is concerned that any companies it insures have strong environmental, health, and safety programs in place. For each company insured, the insurer aims to understand the risks—where they're concentrated geographically and in which sector of the business. The insurer then judges whether those risks are within its risk tolerance level.

In its 2013 sustainability report, The Hartford outlined a variety of opportunities that come with its growing understanding of climate change, including creating new insurance products to meet new needs, "establishing itself as a recognized leader in the assessment and management of climate change-related risks," investing in renewable energy opportunities or "the provision of climate-related risk mitigation services," and "establishing itself as an employer and insurer of choice by demonstrating its commitment to responsible energy use and management and GHG reduction."[12]

Opportunities

Even as climate change poses risk, increased knowledge and understanding of climate change may give rise to a number of opportunities for The Hartford. Greater understanding of the climate change mechanism will lead to more sensitive pricing capability, allowing The Hartford to more effectively match risk to price. In addition, greater understanding and public recognition of climate change may both (a) increase the demand for our insurance products and the willingness to

(continued)

---

[12]The Hartford. (2013). "The Hartford's Sustainability Report 2013." Accessed January 4, 2016. http://www.thehartford.com/sites/thehartford/files/sustainability-report-2013.pdf.

meet our pricing terms and conditions and (b) create opportunities for The Hartford to bring a wider variety of insurance products to market to meet customer needs.

As additional information is developed pointing to increased frequency and severity of weather-related catastrophes, we expect to see more public policy attention paid to such risk mitigation techniques as better land use planning, improved building codes and more rigid enforcement, combined with eliminating subsidies and other incentives that promote development in areas most exposed to natural disasters. The Hartford sees an opportunity in establishing itself as a recognized leader in the assessment and management of climate change-related risks, its commitment to responsible energy use and management and GHG reduction."[1]

As a variety of sectors seek to respond to the challenges and opportunities of climate change—for example, through the generation of renewable energy or through the provision of climate-related risk mitigation services—The Hartford may also benefit from these investment opportunities.

Finally, The Hartford sees opportunity in establishing itself as an employer and insurer of choice by demonstrating its commitment to responsible energy use and management and GHG reduction. The Hartford values its reputation as a responsible corporate citizen and will strive to preserve and enhance that reputation in the area of environmental stewardship.

---

[1]The Hartford. 2013. "The Hartford's Sustainability Report 2013." Accessed January 4, 2016. http://www.thehartford.com/sites/thehartford/files/sustainability-report-2013.pdf.

Internal Resilience and Enterprise Risk Management (ERM): Business Continuity and Risk Management for Catastrophe, Operations, Finance

The Hartford gives plenty of thought to its internal risk tolerance, too. During Hurricane Sandy, as during other recent storms the company, headquartered, as its name belies, in Hartford, Connecticut, "didn't miss a beat," said Bruns. That's because the insurer does have practices in place to accommodate its own potential risks, which have been put to the test during extreme weather in recent years.

For instance, many employees work from home—and all are connected through cell phones and laptop computers—so in severe weather, few people drive to The Hartford's headquarters or other offices. During a 2014 snowstorm, just 253 employees out of 5,000 showed up, while the others worked from home with little interruption. Or, if a storm causes a power outage at home, employees can come to the office to work.

The company also maintains two backup data centers and is moving increasingly to the cloud, which is considered to be more energy efficient. Such precautions and practices fall under the company's business continuity processes and IT office, which, together with internal risk management and catastrophe risk procedures comprise its resilience approach in case of severe weather. Part of that approach also involves scenario planning and practice, such as a fire drill at least once a year.

As an insurer, The Hartford's core business is managing risk. The company manages its risk through a series of steps, starting with its approach to emergency response management (ERM), which broadly covers risks that affect the organization and its strategy—including its exposure to severe weather events, in addition to political, operational, technological, regulatory and other risk.

Insurance is among the earliest sectors to adopt a broad look at risk because "that's how we make our profit," explained Bruns. "If we manage [risk] well, we do [make a profit], and if not, we don't," based on exposure to losses from property, liability, mortality, longevity, and other perils covered under the company's policies.

While climate change might affect all such risks, in the context of ERM, "'severe weather events' [are] almost synonymous with climate change, because that is the manifestation of climate change that potentially affects our company's bottom line," Bruns added.

Beyond ERM, the company follows several steps when considering and responding to risks, he explained:

- "how we respond to our customers who suffer a loss because of the risk" of severe weather events,
- "how we price our insurance to make sure we cover the risks, plus a small profit,"
- "what we do as a company to protect ourselves from severe weather risks," (the internal business resiliency piece)
- "how we reduce our own carbon footprint to help contribute to a solution,"
- "how we make investments to contribute [to global carbon reduction]," (green investments)
- "how we create new products to help our customers go green," such as insuring the renewable energy sector.

Finally, the company manages the risk of its own investments, which are mainly conservative, credit investments, concentrated mostly in Treasuries and other government (e.g., municipal) bonds and commercial paper.

Layered Risk Management

Another way to understand the company's overall risk management approach is through its internal management hierarchy, which falls under the aegis of the Chief Risk Officer (CRO), part of The Hartford's executive leadership, along with the CEO, COO, General Counsel, and other top company officers. The CRO's job is mainly to ensure the company takes on an "appropriate" level of risk and manages it effectively, especially during crises.

Reporting to the CRO are three risk officers, each representing a critical risk factor to the organization—operational risk, insurance risk, and financial risk.

Operational risk includes all that pertains to operations of an insurance company, including functions like ensuring that claims are dealt with promptly and correctly, or that customer service representatives across the country know the company's products. Insurance Risk includes exposure to losses from risk to property, liability, mortality, longevity, and other perils covered under The Hartford's policies. Finally, financial risk includes risks to the assets the company invests in to ensure money is there when customers' claims arrive (including liquidity, interest rate, equity, foreign exchange, and credit risks). The insurer mainly buys financial instruments that pay a return, so funds will be on-hand when customers file a claim. In its CDP report, the company writes:

> We believe that superior risk management, reduced carbon emissions and paper use and attendant savings, enhanced insurance product offerings, and affinity partnerships with environmental groups will help over time differentiate us from our competitors. Long term, The Hartford believes that a growing number of customers interested in reducing their greenhouse gas emissions and generally being more environmentally friendly will create growing business opportunities for insurers. How this is gaining strategic advantage over competitors: Competition in property casualty insurance is intense. Companies are constantly looking for ways to differentiate themselves in the marketplace. We believe that companies that themselves demonstrate a strong, comprehensive, and sustained approach to environmental stewardship and offer appropriate products at the appropriate price can build a green insurance brand. Also, in the war for talent, companies that can demonstrate a serious commitment to environmental stewardship are better positioned to attract and engage talented employees.[13]

As with other companies profiled in this book, The Hartford also encourages employee engagement to advance its own resilience approach. Just as the insurer's concern with climate was initiated by its internal counsel general, so, too, the company relies on employees to suggest ways forward on climate resilience. What's more, soliciting employees' thoughts on improving also incentivizes employees to reduce emissions by involving them in the larger company process—much as offering employees free charging for electric vehicles involves them in advancing the company's overall emission reduction goals.

One powerful example is the Harvest, The Hartford's internal suggestion box soliciting employees' thoughts on how the company can save

---

[13]CDP. (2015). "CDP 2015 Climate Change 2015 Information Request: The Hartford Financial Services Group, Inc." Accessed January 4, 2016. http://www.thehartford.com/sites/thehartford/files/2015-CDP-projectsubmission.pdf.

money, avoid a problem, or become more efficient. After the employee fills out a form, it's reviewed, and if deemed a good idea, implemented. For instance, a few years ago, an employee in the claims division suggested that after an extreme weather event, rather than pay for debris removal from destroyed buildings to go to landfill, the insurer could work with Habitat for Humanity to see if some of the debris—wood, cabinets, appliances—might be of use. Now, rather than pay a garbage company to dispose of the debris, The Hartford has implemented a process so that when there's an extreme weather event, the claims handlers reach out to Habitat to see what may be useful to the organization first.

Risk, Investment, Management

Taken together, these activities add up to risk management, the main business of insurers. As part of its climate risk, the company looks at its investments—and in investing, the company looks at climate risk. Investments critical to insurers are based not just on revenue (from charges to customers, minus payouts) but also on investing those charges, so there will be money on hand when a customer files a claim.

To its credit, the company is thinking about the relationship between investment and climate very carefully. In its 2014 Annual Report,[14] The Hartford explains its risks—and opportunities—as an investor, and how these may be affected by climate: since the company holds mainly fixed-income assets, its main risks are credit-related, and their credit-worthiness may change with climate change, which may affect regulations, fuel supply, and technology developments, effects of extreme weather on issuers. These factors may make some investments more or less attractive. Climate change can also affect investments in fixed assets, such as real estate, changing the value in various locations, the insurer explains.[15]

---

[14]The Hartford. (2016). "The Hartford Quarterly Results." https://ir.thehartford.com/financial-information/quarterly-results/qr-2016.

[15]Statement of the Climate Change. (2016). The Hartford. http://www.thehartford.com/our-company/statement-on-climate-change.

Investment and Risk

The foregoing discussion has focused primarily on the climate change-related risks to which The Hartford is exposed through the sale of insurance products. As a diversified financial services company, The Hartford is exposed to both climate change-related risks and opportunities in its capacity as an investor.

The Hartford's general account investment portfolio holds predominantly fixed-income assets. Therefore, its primary risks are credit-related: corporate and sovereign debt obligations, commercial real estate mortgage loans, and a variety of other fixed-income securities. Nonetheless, the global and regional consequences of climate change play a role in our evaluation of the creditworthiness of specific issuers and industries. Risk (and opportunity) factors include the following:

- Changes in regulatory regimes (e.g., emissions controls, technology mandates);
- Changes in supply/demand characteristics for fuel (e.g., coal, oil, natural gas);
- Advances in low-carbon technology and renewable energy development;
- Effects of extreme weather events on the physical and operational exposure of industries and issuers.

Such risk factors may influence investment strategies and decisions in a variety of ways. As noted, government regulation may have negative or positive consequences for certain industries. For example, increasingly stringent regulation on stack emissions of coal-fired technologies will increase the costs of existing technologies and affect coal economics. More generally, government legislation directed at polluting industries must be scrutinized for the impact on each industry's economics. As polluting industries become more expensive to finance, other low-carbon and renewable energy sources are expected to benefit from increased demand and potential government subsidies.

(continued)

Climate change may have a direct impact on certain investments. For example, commercial real estate in certain locations may become less desirable due to climate change effects (e.g., rising sea levels, increased hurricane severity), negatively affecting a property's value as collateral for a commercial mortgage loan. Similarly, climate changes of a regional nature can influence the inflation outlook and/or creditworthiness of specific emerging market issuers (e.g., reduction in rainfall can cause food prices to rise, increasing inflation).

Finally, The Hartford recognizes that the combination of consumer demand, legislative and regulatory activity, and technological advancement may create substantial opportunities to promote environmentally responsible activity while at the same time enhancing value for The Hartford's shareholders.[13]

---

[13]Statement of the Climate Change. 2016. The Hartford. http://www.thehartford .com/our-company/statement-on-climate-change.

Conclusion

From Risk to Resilience: Managing Risk

As an insurer, The Hartford is steeped in risk: the company takes on the risks of others while managing its own—from enterprise-wide risk, to operational, insurance, regulatory, and financial risks. All are affected by climate risk (and some affect climate risk), as the company explains in its reports.

As a risk-centered business, The Hartford also has shown resilience, in seeking the upside of the risks—opportunities to insure new industries, to create new products, and to respond to new markets. It has developed an internal climate resilience approach that includes business continuity elements, such as off-site data backup, employee opportunities to work off-site, and renewable energy sources (including a solar array on the roof of its building in Windsor, Connecticut).

The Hartford insures against catastrophes, while learning from them how better to manage and respond to such events—even looking for better ways not just to insure but to instruct customers. The company's catastrophe vans are at the ready and continually upgraded. In response to the catastrophe of Hurricane Sandy, the insurer did its own research on small businesses affected by the storm and learning what they might need in future (such as better data backup strategies). As a result, the company surveyed customers and updated its site, incorporating lessons learned into its advice to small business customers.

What the Customer Needs: Learning from Experience

The Hartford's experience with small business after Sandy also illustrates the company's eagerness to learn from experience, to proactively inform itself about what some of its customers suffered, what they might need, and what they might recommend to others. As a key market for the insurer, small business was an important sector to study the hurricane's aftermath, particularly since Mom and Pop stores were among the hardest hit by the storm.

While informing itself about its customers' experiences, The Hartford also asked what small business owners would recommend to others as precautionary measures for future extreme events. The company also has a catastrophe information center on its website.

What's Good for the Customer: New Products for New Markets

The Hartford's concern to stay ahead of potential climate risks has led it to pioneer new products for new markets—a strategy already producing rewards, financially and environmentally. Insuring the renewable energy business is one key example. The company's 11 climate-related products— from insurance for hybrid vehicles and electric fleets to products that incentivize customers to build to more sustainable, climate-resilient standards after severe weather events—illustrate its can-do, innovative spirit in providing customers new products for a changing climate. Those products translate into market advantage for the insurer as a first mover, while growing revenue. Such products also help the customer cut greenhouse gases, reducing climate impacts.

Do-it-Yourself-First: Resilience from the Inside Out

Like Citibank, The Hartford has seen the value in self-testing new products before offering them to the wider market. The company has a growing list of employees who own EVs and is incentivizing them by installing four additional charging stations at its facilities (bringing the total to 12), where employees can recharge gratis. They are also entitled to the EV premium discount. The insurer is greening its fleet and converting 15 percent of its vehicles to hybrids. The company also now offers insurance incentives to both business and individual customers who use electric vehicles.

Like others profiled in this book, The Hartford has also learned that employees can be enthusiastically enlisted to find ways to improve the company's larger environmental initiatives, including climate initiatives. The insurer now solicits their ideas and includes them on its prestigious environment committee.

The value spreads beyond dollars; these moves reduce GHGs for both The Hartford and its customers, which helps with cutting carbon in the atmosphere generally—a positive move for everyone, everywhere. What's more, like Citibank, which took daring and innovative steps, including financial, to improve energy efficiency (most notably in its London data center) and plans to promote its new energy efficiency financing tools to customers, The Hartford has experienced firsthand the relative value of using hybrid vehicles and encouraging EV use among its employees before passing on similar incentives to its customers.

Incentivizing —and Rewarding—Behavior

Incentivizing customers by offering better premiums doesn't stop with electric vehicles. There are also incentives for green homes, such as green equipment breakdown coverage, that allows customers to replace broken appliances, like refrigerators, with systems that have environmental certification. What's more, not only do customers save money on these investments over time, the company potentially pays fewer claims and sells many more of such policies—while the climate, too, benefits from the process.

Investing in Climate

The Hartford's investment doesn't stop with these innovative products for new markets. As an insurance company, The Hartford functions by investing the money from customers' policy fees in financial products that ensure the company has funds on hand to pay claims. The company is increasingly considering the risks of climate—including more abstract connections, like changing regulation—in making its investment decisions. Likewise, The Hartford is considering the consequences of potential climate events or conditions, like extreme weather, on its investments, including looking at how climate (along with other climate-related conditions, such as changing effects on creditworthiness of bonds) might affect such investments. It amounts to investing in a lower-carbon future.

CHAPTER 5

Communicating Change, Collaborating on Climate

IBM: The Power of Data-Driven Partnership

Unlike previous chapters, which mainly addressed internal approaches business is taking to affect climate resilience, this one primarily looks at how one company, IBM, is using processes developed internally to work with the public sector on achieving resilience—in this case, a large community affected by Hurricane Sandy.

Until recently, the focus for the private sector has been preparedness for disruptions of climate change, but private and public sector communication, cooperation, and collaboration are essential if we're to alter our behavior significantly enough to better avert or prepare for risks that can often lead to calamity.

Toward this end, how is information—specifically data—best gathered, stored, and shared? How can it be used to alert people—whether in companies or communities—to potential risks, some that may be fast approaching?

Can we use new forms of information sharing, such as new social media tools, to better engage stakeholders, whether individuals or groups, internal to the organization or outside? Can we create processes to better assess risks—whether long term or immediate, anticipated or not—and thus offer organizations—communities, companies, nonprofits, and others—greater lead time to make decisions based on possible scenarios?

This chapter explores how one community, already badly affected by climate, may better understand how to motivate diverse stakeholders to work together and reduce potential harm from climate events ahead. It investigates how clear communication can lead to awareness, engagement, cooperation, and collaboration among stakeholder groups.

The chapter also explores how companies can transfer some of their internal policies, processes, and technologies to other organizations and stakeholders that can allow them to better share information, assess climate risk, and make decisions in the face of uncertainty—and, in turn, how these groups may transfer some of this experience back to IBM.

Building Resilient Communities: Untangling the Data, Connecting the Dots

The aftermath of 2012's Hurricane Sandy unveiled an uncanny underside to New York State's Suffolk County on suburban Long Island—home to world-renowned ocean-side neighborhoods like the Hamptons.

It's not just that the area was vulnerable to storm surge. Nor was the damage and destruction to tens of thousands of buildings the only sign of devastation from the storm.

What emerged in the aftermath was deeper recognition of an alarming, pre-existing problem exacerbated by Sandy: nitrogen contamination of the County's water supply. Not only is such contamination potentially a public health hazard, it also erodes natural barricades, like wetlands, that guard against storm surges.[1] What's more, in a county of 1.5 million residents and 5 million visitors annually—many of whom come to enjoy the Atlantic coastal beaches—the local economy, too, depends on a healthy water system.

So concerned were County officials that they applied for a grant from IBM's pro bono Smarter Cities program, which sends teams of IBM experts to investigate emerging issues, often environmental, facing modern communities as the world's population expands in urban areas.

Though the odds of winning a grant were stacked against the County due to the number of applications, it won—along with just 15 other cities and counties selected in 2014—bringing the total number of grantees between 2011 and 2014 to 116 (out of 500 applicants).

---

[1]New York State Department of Environmental Conservation. (2014). "Nitrogen Pollution and Adverse Impacts on Resilient Tidal Marshlands: NYS DEC Technical Briefing Summary." Accessed April 22, 2014. http://www.dec.ny.gov/docs/water_pdf/impairmarshland.pdf.

The prize: a team of six senior IBM professionals—including water, data, and community engagement experts—from around the world deployed to work with the County for three weeks to help diagnose the complex breadth and depth of the problem and recommend potential solutions. IBM values each pro bono engagement at $500,000.

Recognizing that two thirds of the world's population will live in cities by 2050, IBM's Smarter Cities program, launched in 2011, grew out of its "Smarter Planet" discussion, initiated in 2008. According to the company's introduction to its findings on Suffolk, that conversation centers on "how the planet is becoming smarter," through intelligent insights gained from an emerging data avalanche from what previously had been assumed to be ordinary things—cars, clothes, power grids, buildings, and more.

Virtually all the Smarter Cities projects involve learning about the type and scope of data relevant to the local context—gathering, sharing, sorting, or even discarding data. In some cases, the data is available but not captured, in other cases, there's an overwhelming amount of data. Often, the IBM team's advice to the community involves helping to process or even dispose of excess data, helping the community to understand which data are relevant, working with the data to anticipate or predict vulnerabilities and potential challenges, and separating the vital information from the data "noise."

In Suffolk County, a key challenge already recognized by officials, NGOs, and others, was to identify current roadblocks, potential risks, and possible strategies to mitigate nitrogen contamination and its effects on the County's water supply to bolster resilience—environmental, economic, health, and otherwise—in the face of potentially more frequent and intense weather events from a changing climate for Long Island communities.

IBM was asked to provide recommendations on how to improve water quality by upgrading data management and sharing, better coordinating agencies and stakeholders, and developing short- and long-term strategic plans for wastewater management.

Among the key issues examined by the IBM team were: the County's water contamination problem and its sources; data systems and data gaps that contribute to confusing information and poor communication;

public sector complexity, economic effects of the issue, and recommendations for potential solutions to the problem of possible nitrogen contamination.

Smarter Cities, Companies, People

While IBM's Smarter Cities program is philanthropic, the company benefits in at least three key ways from projects such as that in Suffolk County—more successful communities, employees who become more proficient and culturally literate become stronger leaders, and greater insight for IBM into potential new markets and commercial solutions.

In the case of Suffolk County, some of the company's top talent in data, water management, and community engagement from around the world tackled a mounting global problem: community resilience to intensifying effects of a changing climate, in this case heightened by Superstorm Sandy. Importantly, too, some recommendations mirror the kinds of risk management procedures IBM follows itself, with its suppliers, and for its customers (See box: Risk Assessment and Resilience).

Indeed, some of what the experts suggested for Suffolk parallels IBM's own approaches to resilience including an emphasis on

Risk Assessment and Resilience

IBM's approach to resilience isn't limited to its work with Suffolk County or within its Smart Cities program. On the contrary, the company has long viewed risk—the complement of resilience—as a key issue to manage, ramping up its assessment process in 2009. After the market crash the year before, IBM realized that it needed to do more to protect against potential risks of all sorts, including more careful assessment of the risk that suppliers potentially pose both to IBM and to themselves. A new risk offering will also help customers manage their risk.

Recognizing the risks inherent in doing business, IBM continually assesses and reassesses those in its business units and puts plans in place to address them. However, with the rapid growth of global sourcing, the company began to identify mounting risks, often cumulative. By 2010, IBM's procurement base had reached about $40 billion per year. (Due to divestment of some businesses, like hardware, the company's procurement base has dropped to a still hefty $30 billion from 17,000 suppliers.)

That year, in order to manage the risk process consistently at the enterprise level, IBM codified its enterprise risk management initiatives in a new C-suite position, that of Chief Risk Officer (CRO). That function is finding its way to more and more companies, as the proliferation of risks—anticipated and unanticipated—of various sorts, including climate-related risks, becoming more vital to operative success.

Significantly, much of the company's risk management approach grew out of its corporate environmental policy, established in 1971. Since then, expectations, notably on the part of customers and investors, of what companies should do to behave responsibly toward the environment and society have risen substantially, with the issue of responsible supply chains of particular concern.

As stakeholders started to raise such concerns and probe beyond the environmental and social risks internal to IBM to ask about how its suppliers handle those risks—and what IBM does to help guide them—the company began to look more deeply into how, or even if, its sourcing companies managed risk. With mounting stakeholder demand came greater internal interest in understanding and managing the company's supply chain.

Indeed, IBM now views risk management as a critical part of running a business sustainably. Explained IBM's Global Procurement Project Executive Louis Ferretti: "Sustainability and risk management are conjoined and inseparable. When you talk about sustainability, that includes shortages of raw materials, clean water, and air, which are requirements of manufacturing, you need to understand the risks of doing business, and that spills into the supply chain and the sustainability process. So if a company doesn't have a sustainability plan, then that's an enterprise risk management concern."

For IBM, as for an increasing number of companies, resilience is understood as the flip side of risk, Ferretti said. In its supply chain, the

(continued)

company first assesses the level of risk it thinks exists in doing business with a supplier, looking at both the supplier and the supplier's own supply chain.

However, the risk assessment doesn't evaluate the supplier's resilience capacity. To understand that, the company engages with the supplier in business continuity planning, helping IBM to determine the supplier's level of preparedness for disruptions of many sorts. "The supplier could be very good on risk, delivery and quality, but how do we know it has sufficient recovery capacity or continuity plans in place?" explained Ferretti.

To ascertain the supplier's potential resilience, IBM engages in a series of questions about the business, probing how prepared it is for a host of potential outages and disruptions, including those affecting transportation, power, and employee among others. Various climate, social, or political challenges exist in different places, such as typhoons in Asia.

Also included in the assessment is a series of questions about the supplier's business continuity management plan, including its IT work-recovery preparedness, alternate locations for critical functions or data backup, testing scenarios, potential absenteeism, and preparedness for health emergencies and for overall functioning of the organization.

Based on the answers, IBM determines a rating of the supplier's resilience level, recognizing that some remediation may be needed to bolster it.

Importantly, the supplier risk assessment mirrors IBM's own risk assessment process for every business unit. Each is asked to identify critical processes and develop a business continuity plan that's documented, reviewed, and tested, according to a standard set of scenarios. Real-life problems, including lessons learned from extreme weather events and other continuity plans, are often added to the list as they occur.

The procurement organization, like all critical businesses, has a management system and reports to the larger enterprise risk function on metrics, new threats or risks, with periodic reviews quarterly and yearly. However, the company is continuously monitoring situations, such as typhoons, rather than waiting for a crisis, to re-evaluate risks.

In the supply chain and procurement area, big data and analytics are key to risk assessment. The unit's risk tool or TRA (Total Risk Assessment), examines five dimensions for the supplier, including: country and region; shipping hub; supplier risk at the enterprise level; supplier risk at the site level, including what is made for IBM at that site.

To ensure its own business continuity within each of the five areas, IBM asks each supplier a host of questions to collect data then used in an algorithm to determine potential impact from various risks, ultimately weighing impact and likelihood to determine a risk rating. The company also subscribes to external data sources to get input on information about a range of issues like shipping, corruption, employment or political situations, discounting some depending on the region.

Once completed, the risk assessment doesn't change dramatically month to month or even year to year. However, "What does change is weather, politics, labor—and that happens every day," explained Ferretti, so IBM must monitor potential disruptions continuously. To deal with frequent changes, IBM uses an active, real-time alert management system it developed to learn about anything that happens anywhere in the world every day that could affect a supplier, examining what the company is doing to potentially preempt a disruption and recover.

IBM is currently using its Watson capability technology, based partly on natural language and partly on artificial intelligence, that can search and analyze unstructured data—representing a full 80 percent of all data—to develop further dimensions of risk prevention. The system was first used in projects for large companies and institutions, particularly in health care and medicine.

The company is now using it for internal purposes to get a clearer picture of the potential impact of climatic events and better assess what actions to take and what decisions to make. So, for instance,

(continued)

Watson might be able to analyze data from a variety of sources, such as Twitter or the US Naval weather forecasts, to help the company better track individual storms and how they may affect supply chains. Information could be updated on category of storm, speed, and where and when it's likely to hit. This is the kind of thing the company hopes to do more of with its work with the Weather Company (see Smarter Cities, Companies, People section in body of chapter for more detail).

redundancy in data backups to help ensure business continuity and use of selected social media outlets for helpful alerts before, during, and after calamities.

IBM's recent partnership with Twitter may help to augment the growing communications component of climate resilience—as may the company's new partnership on weather data with The Weather Company, which absorbs 20 terabytes daily from weather stations, satellites, and other sources, and is used to populate information for weather apps on Apple devices and others.[2] Weather data will be sent to IBM's artificial intelligence and other analysis tools to deliver "a new service for business: detailed weather information and insights for decision-making." IBM reports that "weather is perhaps the single largest external swing factor in business performance—responsible for an annual economic impact of nearly half a trillion dollars in the US alone."[3] One likely application is auto insurance. For instance, the service could allow the insurer to send early warnings for hail storms via text messages to policy holders.

Finally, in the company's external Superstorm Sandy Report, IBM explained that its research arm, in collaboration with universities based in Finland and Portugal:

---

[2]Lohr, Steve. (2015). "IBM introduces Twitter-fueled data services for businesses." *The New York Times*, March 17, 2015. http://bits.blogs.nytimes.com/2015/03/17/ibm-introduces-twitter-fueled-data-services-for-business/?_r=0

[3]IBM. (2015). "IBM and The Weather Company Partner to Bring Advanced Weather Insights to Business." Accessed January 4, 2015. https://www-03.ibm.com/press/us/en/pressrelease/46446.wss.

developed a new technology called Crisis Tracker, a social media analytics Web service pilot project that captures and classifies Twitter feeds real time. As a pilot project, Crisis Tracker was trained on the social media traffic in the wake of the storm. Crisis Tracker captured a subset of all tweets about Sandy, clustering them into like "stories," which could then be evaluated by volunteers for veracity and geocoding.

Processed stories appeared on a GIS interface, showing the locations that tweets were associated with. The objective of this study was to show how tweets could be informative about shortages of food or water, disrupted utilities, road closures, violence, building damage, and so on. When plotted to a map, the information can be used by decision makers as they try to address urgent needs following disaster. Nineteen IBM volunteers signed up for the pilot and helped classify and validate tweets. Through this pilot, IBM Research gained valuable data to assess and improve Crisis Tracker, putting it in line for possible deployment as a grant to partners in future disaster events.[4]

Clams, Climate and Wetlands Reclamation: Water–Data Nexus for Climate Resilience

With its population of 1.5 million, "larger than 11 states in the country individually," Suffolk County has a lot of people to protect—not just during emergencies like Hurricane Sandy, but all the time, explained Sarah Lansdale, Director of Planning for the County.

Because of its concern for its population and its vulnerable location along the Atlantic coastline, the County "has been at the forefront of coastal resilience efforts for decades and poured millions of dollars into the restoration of the clam industry," she explained. Over time, the County "realized that investing in reclamation of shellfish beds wasn't solving the [nitrogen] problem or the source. No matter how many oysters we plant, it won't keep up with the nitrogen influx. We had to

[4]IBM. (2013). "IBM Humanitarian Disaster Response for Superstorm Sandy 2012: External Report November 2013." IBM. November 2013.

look at the source of the problem." After Superstorm Sandy, the County "lost a significant amount of wetlands, [which had already been] eroding over the years because of nitrification," Lansdale said, adding that, "New York State estimates an 18 to 36 percent loss [in wetland area] from 1974 to 2000."[5]

The County also now knows that 69 percent of the nitrogen load driving the wetlands loss is from septic tanks and cesspools, the sole form of wastewater treatment in the County.[6] Septic systems that have a holding tank and a leaching pool help to clean the wastewater by removing solids, and in some cases may marginally reduce the amount of nitrogen. A cesspool performs the same function but acts more like a colander, with cement blocks stacked on top of each other acting as a holding tank, Lansdale explained. She added: "Cesspools (or leaching pools) are pits into which concrete, brick or cement block walls have been placed. Wastewater flows into the cesspool and drains or "percolates" into the soil through the perforated walls."[7] She explained:

> In Sandy, you literally had people's systems floating in the water and saw the waste in the water for days. The flooding lasted for several days, and once the systems are flooded, then it takes months for the bacteria in the system to [dissipate so that the system can] reestablish itself and work properly.

The combined problems were a large part of the impetus for the "Reclaim Our Water" initiative launched by the Suffolk County Executive in 2014, which "identified that nitrogen, mainly from [cesspools and septic

---

[5]See New York State Department of Environmental Conservation. (2014). "Nitrogen Pollution and Adverse Impacts on Resilient Tidal Marshlands NYS DEC Technical Briefing Summary." Accessed April 22, 2014. http://www.dec.ny.gov/docs/water_pdf/impairmarshland.pdf.

[6]Kinney E.L., and I. Valiela. (2011). "Nitrogen Loading to Great South Bay: Land Use, Sources, Retention, and Transport from Land to Bay." *Journal of Coastal Research* 27(4): 672–686.

[7]ABC Cesspool and Septic Pumping. (2014). "What is a Septic Tank? What is a Cesspool?" Accessed September 23, 2015. http://abccesspoolandsepticpumping.com/septic-tank-cesspool/.

systems], was polluting surface waters and leading to degradation of our wetlands—which act as a line of defense for the population that lives on the coast, especially during coastal events like storm surges," Lansdale explained. "Wetlands act as a sort of sponge or break as surges approach land and reduce velocity and height of the surge."

The nitrification of the water supply was already disturbing because the County gets its drinking water from the ground. "The Department of Health Services has been monitoring wells throughout the County, but since Sandy, we've looked at the nitrogen issue in relation to the quality of our wetlands," too, Lansdale said, mainly because they protect against effects of storms.

After Sandy, the County began consulting slosh maps and aerial photos along with future projections of sea level rise (mainly from Columbia University's Goddard School of Science and Technology). Officials also looked at County maps and began to identify "relations between the flooding from Sandy, and where the septic tanks and cesspools are, along with where groundwater is 10 feet deep or less," Lansdale said, finding that of 360,000 tanks and pools, 209,000 were in areas determined to be a priority for upgrades.

The combined realizations about water quality, wetland vulnerability, and probable extreme future weather events led to the County's bid for the IBM grant. Explained Lansdale: "Our hope was that IBM could work with the County and leaders throughout Suffolk to clearly identify the problem and begin to develop a framework of possible strategies and actions to work toward in a coordinated fashion."

Depth of a Water Problem

Once Suffolk secured the grant, the IBM experts came in to analyze the problems in more depth. Jan Bowen, IBM Executive Partner and Water Industry Leader in Global Business Services, flew in from England, along with five other team members from other parts of the company—and around the world—with specialties including data, analytics, supply chain, and community engagement. When Bowen arrived, the County had already:

recognized and articulated that they have an issue with excess nitrogen in the ground, and therefore in the groundwater, and that contamination of the water has effects with regard to the island['s ability] to cope with environmental [disruptions], like storms and flooding.

One of the main causes of nitrogen is [the] high proportion of septic solutions on the island that aren't designed to treat nitrogen. The water [from septic systems] goes into the ground to an aquifer, which the water company treats for drinking water.

One of the misconceptions in the community, Bowen said, was that the septic tanks were failing. However, that wasn't the case, "because they weren't designed to [treat nitrogen]. There are septic solutions that can treat nitrogen, but most in existence today don't." One of the challenges, she said, is converting people to that new solution.

As a water expert, she was able to articulate that the effects of nitrogen can be good, in that nitrogen helps plants grow. But when there's an excessive amount, as in Suffolk County, there can be negative impacts: "First, the rain falls into the ground, and moves through the ground to the aquifer. It takes a few years to go through the land until the water is treated to make it safe to drink." If it is heavily contaminated, the water is very costly to treat, Bowen added, and in the case of Suffolk County, the cost is in the billions.

And, when the water goes into the ground, on the way to the streams and the ocean, "the second major impact is on the marshlands[8] that protect the bay. Those have been dissipated [in Suffolk], and there's a concern in some areas that too much algae will grow, which affects the fish and other ocean life." What's more, she said, the marshes themselves act as protection:

If you get a [storm like] Sandy, because [plants in marshlands] hold the land there through the roots. But if they're lost, then you get

---

[8]Marshlands are wetlands that are continually or frequently inundated with water, according to the EPA. EPA. (2012). "Marshes." Accessed October 10, 2012. http://water.epa.gov/type/wetlands/marsh.cfm.

erosion and that affects the ecosystem and the land and everything. Suffolk had worked with a range of stakeholders and researched and noted the deterioration with universities and other organizations, like The Nature Conservancy. For sure, something as severe as Sandy didn't do any good. The storm didn't cause the nitrogen excess, but it had detrimental effects on the whole situation.

IBM's Key Recommendations: Water, Data, Engagement

IBM came up with a number of key recommendations for Suffolk, of which the top three to boost county resilience included addressing water, data, and community engagement.

A first priority for Suffolk is to "select the right water solution, something the County had already started," Bowen noted. That includes "identifying what are the different septic solutions and what to do with regard to waste treatment," she said, adding that the County, "shouldn't do that without looking at the full water cycle, because they're interrelated. You have to make sure you have the right technology integrated into the larger situation."

A second priority was to protect against loss of data and improve the quality, accessibility, compatibility, and coherence of data. The County "needs to understand the impacts of their actions, so they need to access and look at trends over time; the challenge is getting hold of the information and putting it in a form that's usable to different organizations so that they can manage and share it more intelligently," Bowen explained.

A third priority was to engage the community and its various stakeholder groups to raise local awareness so that solutions could be selected and implemented. Bowen noted that much of this engagement is very personal, because "it involves people making a decision to dig up a garden and take out something that's been there for 30 years and put something else in." There's a cost and disturbance to that, and the cost born by individuals is ultimately one of the biggest challenges the County faces:

So how that's funded and what options are there for funding is critical. All sorts of things are possible, but it's still a $7 or 8 billion number. And in some cases, it's about connecting people to sewers, not moving [away] from septic, so it affects the infrastructure around streets. These are complex questions. The crux of the problem is that hundreds of thousands of properties aren't connected to the sewer, and it's not the right answer to all cases, because there are very different demographics around the county.

County Planning Director Lansdale noted that Suffolk had already been awarded $383 million to connect 10,500 homes to the sewage system, the largest investment in infrastructure to Suffolk in 40 years.

Community Resilience: Awareness and Economics

Finally, there's the question of community resilience, which entails raising awareness of water quality and use, as well as understanding the business implications of resilience measures to the community, Bowen explained. In raising awareness of water quality, she said:

> Until you have a conversation with the community, they don't think about water. [Residents] flush and forget it. You don't think about what happens to the water before it arrives at the tap, you just use it. So people are just unaware of the implications, and therefore they don't know whether it's good to maintain septic tanks and all sorts of related issues. The point here is to raise awareness of poor water quality on the lives of those in the community and what they want to do.

The business implication investigation, she continued, "is ongoing. We discussed with Suffolk County other examples in other parts of the world where communities are maintaining beaches and have identified a maximum [number of days] to fish or boat or enjoy other forms of recreation." IBM brought to the County's attention examples of community resiliency planning for small businesses that survive on tourism. "There's a knock-on effect," said Bowen:

> People live there because it's close to the ocean, and visitors come for that, too. So if your economy isn't attracting businesses, then it becomes more and more remote from the direct cause [of the

problem], but you can see a link [between excess nitrogen and economic vitality]. And I think that ultimately the biggest driver here is that if you continue to contaminate the aquifer, you won't be able to provide a safe water source. Suffolk is a long way from that, but ultimately that would have an effect.

Data Tangle: Problem, Solutions—and Cost of Resilience

One of the key reasons Suffolk applied for a grant with IBM was to examine the County's data that serve as indicators for water quality—including data gaps, data sharing, and related issues—explained Lansdale. "One of the recommendations [IBM made] was to establish a framework to identify, visualize, and manage water quality," she said. "As part of the IBM team's engagement, they convened a range of stakeholders, from the water authority to the US Geological Survey, to the US EPA, local towns and the health department."

The team found that "there are places where we overlapped in data collection," said Lansdale, "for instance, in monitoring pharmaceuticals in our drinking water, where the County was doing it, and also the water authority." On the other hand, "there were data gaps," she said, "So, for instance, we don't have unified data that shows whether a house has a septic tank or a cesspool, and there are records that aren't digitized, which could be an important factor [to help prioritize] which homes should be upgraded first."

After speaking with stakeholders, it became clear that "there was a need to establish a data platform that could be shared with stakeholders," she said, including groups as diverse as the US Geological Survey, Suffolk County Department of Health Services, Suffolk County Water Authority, local municipalities, and nonprofit organizations.

IBM's lead team member on the data component of the County's problem was Florida-based Cesar Saavedra, a software systems and data management consultant with years of experience as a developer, along with expertise in customer solutions, software sales, and technology pre-sales.

"I take customer problems and analyze the situation from their data and systems, and try to find the best ways to solve their problems of data integration, often in disaster recovery. There's lots of work in environment," he said.

For the Suffolk County Smarter Cities project, Saavedra served as:

> the tech guy who covered all the data and systems topics. Once the team got there, we realized the problem was much bigger than we originally thought. It wasn't just a data problem—though that was one aspect of the solution we proposed—there was also education, IT more generally, management. These are all areas the County needs to tackle—engagement, execution, finance, a blue print for the future, all wrapped into integrated water management.

Nonetheless, data is crucial to solving the County's problems, Saavedra explained:

> Data is an enabler of a larger plan they need to work on—how to handle water and wastewater—which were disconnected. People thought about them as two separate things. But in a water cycle, they're connected. Water is very cheap there, and people water their lawns a lot, partly because water is so cheap. There's nitrogen on the land, and it shifts into the water table beneath the surface and contaminates the aquifer and coastal water areas, and that affects the marshes that protect the island from harsh weather.

Data is also a critical element of the larger problem facing the County. "Lots of people [interviewed by IBM] had different theories" about the cause of the water problems. A lack of data meant disagreements about the source of the nitrogen among different stakeholder groups, which had prevented them from effective action.

> We also found out that there was systems duplication. For instance, the County has a GIS system, and some townships use a different system or use the County system in different ways. So they couldn't exchange data, which didn't help in understanding the single view, which made it even harder to share data:

Appraisal data was held at the town level, and the County was starting to determine how many houses had septic tanks or cesspools to roll out a plan to alleviate the contamination. But lots of that data was at the town level because when you build a house, the town has to approve that and holds the data. So we realized there was a need for entities to share the data to execute studies or make informed decisions, versus guessing or making an estimate. There was limited data and no standardized way to store it so it was all in different forms, which complicates things.

The situation was similar with the GIS systems, with "one town using ESRI data [and] different data from the County, so they couldn't share data. The lack of common data and a countywide data format was an impediment to sharing" information to better understand and resolve the problem. Exacerbating the situation was the County's use of "one-off applications," said Saavedra:

> They had written their own programs, in Windows or Unix, so there were lots of different ones built in-house by different people. They hadn't bought them off the shelf from a particular company, and the person who had written it and had the knowledge may have left the County. So no one knew how to update it, and so they didn't. Lots of applications were written according to what a specific person knew, and often that was just the simple programs that come when you buy a laptop with Windows—Power Point, Word, and so on—but you shouldn't use that to run your business. For a system your citizens will use, you need enterprise-grade software.

Yet another big problem was data analytics:

> Data reporting and analysis was done by running SQL statements, for instance: select item 1, 2 or 3 from the table and sort it and create a chart or a graph with that. Now you can do that with an analytics tool, like IBM Cognos or predictive analysis.

Instead, the County's approach was mainly "manual, from queries to the database," so the analysis was "very limited and basic. You could do much more with predictive analytics, for instance showing where you might need to build sewers in 10 years, or dig a well, or view current contamination and potential growth—where will we be in 10 years." Of course, "software costs money," says Saavedra:

> but in the long term, you end up saving. So, say, if it costs $10,000, if that helps you better plan wastewater treatment and recovery of environmentally damaged areas and to better protect the County for harsh weather, that will save billions of dollars, because marshes will continue to act as a cushion and protect property.

Yet another solution the team found was that the County could "do a lot of software rationalization," mainly because different organizations had software from different vendors, all with the same function. "They could consolidate that to one, so everyone uses the same system, and that would save money and make the information more consistent, and they could talk to each other," instead of paying for both ESRI and McIntosh.

As if that weren't enough, lots of software applications were being developed by "people who didn't have the background in computer science. They had written the apps on their own time, but programming or systems development wasn't their specialty, which explained why they had so many one-off apps using Windows Access," Saavedra explained.

Data Recommendations

The IBM team came up with five key recommendations to sort through the data tangle: (1) A County-wide IT department and director; (2) a common information model; (3) single-view access to fragmented data; (4) digitization of all data; (5) a backup data center as a disaster recovery preparedness plan. Explained Saavedra:

> The first thing we suggested for the County was to put all the IT departments under a single director. Right now, they have a federated IT department, and the problem in this case is that if they continue to use different systems, that goes against rationalizing and consolidating information and software and software licenses that save money. Also, the current autonomous system

leads to saving data in different formats, making it more difficult to share data.

So we recommended a single, central IT department, with a pool of folks—a database administrator, operators, developers—with a shared pool of resources, so that if one person leaves the County, the knowledge stays with the pool.

The second thing the IBM team recommended was to start working on a common information model.

Instead of tackling everything in a single shot, why not take a couple of data sources you have, whether the chemistry of wells or other information, and work on a common information model, represented the same way across the board?

That recommendation comes with a sensitivity caveat, Saavedra explained:

We understand that some towns have to keep the data. For those cases, we recommend a data federation approach—not for the IT [team], but for the data. Some of that has to stay with the village, so for the data, we recommended to make it look the same, maybe using a master data management approach, so that for the user [at the county level], the data looks like it's all in one place. The back end of the system takes care of data from different sources, but it surfaces as though it comes from a single source. The aim is to synch the data, which stays at different sources.

A third recommendation was that:

any application using fragmented data has to be made to be accessed in a single view application. So, first you have a central IT group, then a common information model, and then you modify the application you wrote to access the common information model.

A fourth recommendation was to start digitizing a lot of information that's still on paper so that various stakeholders could use it in electronic form.

Finally, the team recommended a data disaster recovery approach for preparedness against potential events. That would mean having a second center housing data far away from the main center "so that if that one is destroyed by bad weather, you don't lose the data."

Public, Private Sector Data

Saavedra notes that, while the recommendations are similar to those he works on for the private sector, there are differences in the case of a municipality, which has different government regulations:

> The problems Suffolk had that suggest a common information model using more common enterprise solutions—that very often happens in the private sector. The difference is with government regulations. When it comes to data security, there's the Freedom of Information Act, so if the County gets a request for data to be released, sometimes the data can be denied. They can't share social security numbers or addresses, so all of that has to be accounted for in the solution.
>
> So in the common information model, there are levels of beach contamination, or perhaps the level of nitrogen where people live, if you have a map showing properties, you can't show who owns [which property]. So the data solution has to account for all that. In the private sector, that kind of privacy issue might be more related to credit cards and social security numbers.

Information, Communication, Engagement—and Community Resilience

Building on the data findings and suggestions, the team's third top recommendation was to boost the community's resilience by sharing critical information, using the latest communications platforms, and engaging key stakeholders. "There wasn't a common plan on how to get to what everyone wanted—a vibrant economy, clean water, a healthy population," said IBM team member Kelly Clifton, a Strategy and Analytics Consultant who flew to Suffolk from IBM Global Services in Charlotte, North Carolina.

Talking with many stakeholders, Clifton noticed that, while they all understood there was a growing threat, "what stood out was that everyone had their own idea of what the main problem was—a data problem, a policy issue, a scientific issue—but there wasn't an overarching objective."

The goal of bolstering community resilience grew out of the term "resilience," used in Suffolk mainly in an environmental context in the wake of Sandy, said Clifton. "After the Superstorm [Sandy], the community realized they were vulnerable; they saw the surface ground water issues and that individual septic systems were contributing to this contamination," she recounted:

> It was a wake-up call: "Maybe we're not as resilient to a massive storm as we thought." So, it was partly the environmental piece. But there was also talk among different stakeholders about economic resilience, especially tourism and how to keep people coming back to the community. The longer-term economy became part of the conversation among so many groups with a stake in the matter. They wanted to make sure the sand dunes were there—and the people, too.

Teasing out an engagement approach for the community involved a savvy communications process that brought together various stakeholder groups and built on some of the conclusions about community data that surfaced during the team's work.

Much was revealed during an initial workshop, with an exercise on access to data, whose aim was "to actually see what gaps and overlaps existed within the County itself," she said. "We brought together different stakeholders—County staff and officials, nonprofit groups—and used post-it notes and big white sheets of paper, categorized according to topics like water quality, environmental zoning, land use, human services," allowing stakeholders to visualize the gaps and overlaps.

> Everyone had a pack of post-its and was asked to write down the data they had related to a particular problem or the data they wish they had access to or that they know exists somewhere but haven't seen. It was very interactive, with everyone talking, and there were all these post-its on the wall, and everyone was amazed to see that

one person might have the data they need, and that someone else was missing X, and I can help them find this,

she explained. "So in a very short period of time, the stakeholders could see what they had and didn't have and how they could provide information to others, where the holes were, where there was overlap and the like," she added:

> What that workshop really showed was that mostly, the data was there, so that an initial step in community engagement would be first to get people to see what's there and then talk about how to manage it better. Some data might be missing, but one group didn't know that another group actually had it, or where it was stored, or how to access it. And then some said that it was on paper or in filing cabinets and hard to access and share.

Several umbrella recommendations emerged as part of a way to better engage stakeholders in what would necessarily have to become a collective goal of resilience. For instance, the team recommended that the community use social media to communicate about commonly shared risks or meetings that might affect everyone. "We didn't explicitly give them a strategy for social media," explained Clifton, but suggested that:

> it would be great for them to explore a strategy for it, because it's relatively quick and low cost. It might not be a way to solve the underlying problem, but it could be a good way to try something out. So we suggested a small education program on water quality for school children as a way to test out a strategy to get citizens informed.

In terms of specific tools, the team "mentioned smart phone apps, Facebook and Twitter as ways to share information and then left the County to decide [a social media strategy]," said Clifton. She added that she thought Twitter "would be great, just to communicate information about a town hall meeting on water quality or promotional videos or documentaries and studies from local universities. It's quick and inexpensive."

As for suggesting an engagement approach, the team "recognized that even if the community is vibrant, there needs to be a policy and some procedures to align that engagement with potential action," explained Clifton:

> The community could be very excited and engaged, but we found that in order to actually have impact through engagement, there had to be a governance structure set up to have engagement happen. For instance, there was a discussion about new technologies for septic systems. One individual explained there was a great new technology but couldn't [be implement], because there was a County policy that didn't allow it on a particular part of the coastline. So even if they wanted it, they couldn't have it. So we saw that the community could be engaged and want to do something but that there has to be a two-way street to stream with policy. So we [suggested] linking governance and engagement.

Clifton added that the engagement challenge could be related to general communications challenges when multiple stakeholders are involved. "It seemed with Suffolk that without appropriate institutions and policies, engagement would be difficult to translate to results," she said:

> In this scenario, everyone was engaged, but in a bubble. So if they were able to communicate back and forth quickly and with accurate information and have a structure in place to allow that, then the results would likely turn out better, as in the workshop. We didn't solve the problem in those 30 minutes. It's not a quick fix, but it's a great first step to figure out what's going on.

Clifton acknowledged, too, that some of the challenges might be related to organizational "silos" in a government structure, as in companies or other organizations, including nonprofits, that also participated in the County stakeholder process:

> In some aspects, there were so many stakeholders to be interviewed—scientists, nonprofits—and they all have their own rules and regs and missions. But once they're able to get together and start a dialogue, it was much easier. It's not impossible, even if people are in their own silos, if you're able to break those down,

she noted. How to do that involves what she sees, again, as an overarching common, positive goal:

> You need to make sure your governance structure allows for that kind of information sharing, and you also need to have a positive engagement strategy. We suggested a few things: for engagement using social media, and something similar to a blue flag program that our European colleagues are used to—where a blue flag is set up on a beach that [represents] certain established criteria, like good, safe water quality. We suggested that as positive reinforcement, to attract people for tourism, shopping, patronizing restaurants. You could have it online and [communicate] it through social media to get people excited about the beach. So it's a good way to positively call out good, safe, attractive places.

In approaching resilience and potentially finding ways to bolster it within business, some of the same communications "rules of thumb" from the County experience might prove relevant in companies, where silos often limit information sharing, if unwittingly.

Conclusion

Effective Communications and Engagement

Much of the critical learning for communities and companies alike from IBM's experience guiding Suffolk toward building a resilient community is relatively simple, if harder to enact:

- Reach an overarching goal that the whole community can strive for;
- Understand the underlying problem (in Suffolk's case water, as for so many U.S. areas at risk from rising sea levels, storm surges and floods) and educate the public about it;
- Raise awareness, including the business case and economic reasons for and against potential solutions;
- Search the data you're already collecting and learn how to manage and share it better—perhaps even delete some, while

updating, synching, and properly backing up your systems along the way; and
- Engage the community, including multiple stakeholders, levels of management, demographics, and vested interests.

The goal of community—or business—resilience isn't easily accomplished. But when there's a common understanding that the physical and other changing conditions actually affect everyone—if in different ways—then it may be possible to find a practical way to approach what, at the individual agency level, may appear to be an overwhelming challenge.

In the case of Suffolk County, IBM uncovered three major ways the community might approach these goals, with the aim of building community resilience: (1) boosting awareness, including educating the public about the underlying water problem and helping them understand the potential costs, economic and otherwise; (2) examining the data on the problem—who had, or didn't have what, and how to maximize its use—while minimizing confusion; (3) engaging the community.

Each solution boils down to effective communication.

Such a three-pronged approach might work well not just in Suffolk but in other communities and companies. Importantly, the approach can also work across public and private entities, as is increasingly recognized, not least in the COP 21 Paris agreement, that both must work together collaboratively—and in concert with other sectors, such as NGOs—in order to effect resilience. Indeed, they are beginning to do so. Suffolk County is a case in point, mainly because its key economic engine, tourism, is essential to the livelihood of all who live and work there.

Awareness

In Suffolk County, boosting awareness of the underlying problem—water—and how it was changing over time, is critical to engaging the community. Understanding potential health, economic and larger environmental and safety effects the problem might continue to foster is critical to engaging the community to take action that might lead to resilience.

Awareness-building can take different forms, such as, in the case of Suffolk, simple education programs for children that might have a mushroom effect of enlightening parents. Community examination of costs of change—or of doing nothing—is also a vital part of raising awareness and boosting engagement. Such awareness-building is unlikely to be a one-off exercise. As the community learns more and starts to take action, stakeholders will likely have to learn about local climate changes.

Data

In this day and age of big data, one key to action is to untangle what may be a maze of information, perhaps in different forms, different systems, and in the hands of different people. Sharing data that already exists—rather than creating more—can often be a start, an approach that may entail greater collaboration, such as uncovering unnecessary duplications, exposing one-off applications that may be difficult to share, and updating an old system to use newer analytics that may help predict trends or events to help make decisions. Rationalizing the software—to bring down costs and help make the data more consistent and manageable—is another key. Finally, ensuring there's a backup system for the data in a different place is critical.

In the case of Suffolk County, five key recommendations helped to sort through the data tangle: (1) a central, in this case County-wide IT department and director, to help rationalize and consolidate software and cut costs; (2) a common information model to represent, as much as possible, the same data to different groups or stakeholders; (3) single-view access to fragmented data; (4) digitization of all data, moving away from paper to an electronic format that everyone can share; (5) a data disaster recovery approach to preparedness for potential events, usually a backup data center in a different location, so that, in case the base center is destroyed in bad weather, the data isn't lost.

Engagement

As for engaging the community, some simple recommendations could prove useful to other communities and companies—especially in the early stages of building awareness. In this age of social media, much can be accomplished by using common communications platforms. Many people already use these to share information, so vehicles like Facebook or Twitter and other smart phone apps could be repurposed to let the community know about potential weather changes or critical community meetings. These are quick and low-cost ways to convey potentially vital information.

One way to bring together various stakeholder groups to better understand—and eventually collaborate on boosting—"community resilience" can be to introduce the concept of economic resilience into the equation, tying it to a local environmental issue, as was demonstrated in Suffolk. A straightforward way to get different people and groups to start communicating can be simply to bring them together to talk about who has what information in order to share it better—as demonstrated by the initial meeting IBM organized using simple tools like index cards and white boards. That led to thinking about how better to manage the information and then to more overarching recommendations to help disparate groups eventually embrace a collective, community resilience goal.

Importantly, whether in a community or a business organization, accomplishing a larger goal like resilience is well supported by a policy along with procedures that align engagement to action to achieve the goal. Any overarching policy or governance structure should support fast and easy information sharing to achieve the positive engagement whose ultimate aim is to effect positive change. What's more, sharing and analyzing accurate data is essential for informing policy as well as decision making.

Conclusion

Innovating for Solutions—How, Not If

Our Changing Climate: Inspiring Business Change

The 2015 Conference of the Parties (COP 21) in Paris left little doubt: The question is no longer if business is part of the climate solution, but how.

Even before the Paris meetings, where 196 countries signed an agreement to counter climate change, companies across a wide swath of sectors made commitments to cut emissions, move to renewable energy, and otherwise work to stem climate change. Such business commitments represent a giant step forward on climate adaptation and resilience and augur well for curtailing climate change.

What's more, conversations at COP 21 have illustrated how innovative business approaches to blend traditionally separate functions such as sustainability, mitigation, adaptation, disaster, risk, markets, and investment, can support the fight against climate change. Such conversations also suggest that no one sector, such as government or business, can solve this crisis alone but that all must work together.

The companies profiled in this book provide important clues to the nascent, ongoing efforts of business leaders to improve climate resilience, including approaching risk in a new way.

Over the course of the last decade, climate-related natural disasters have left a lasting impression on the companies profiled. As recounted throughout this book, Hurricane Katrina in New Orleans in August 2005, the Sendai earthquake and tsunami in March 2011 in Japan, the 2012 floods in Thailand, Typhoon Haiyan in the Philippines in 2013, and especially Hurricanes Sandy and Irene on the eastern coast of the United States in 2012, have all played critical roles in awakening business to the risks of our changing climate. Some risks exposed by these events include vulnerabilities in emergency preparedness and operational efficiency; also exposed were the potential rewards of tackling these risks through business adaptation measures.

Likewise, business has not been detached from effects of ongoing weather conditions, such as droughts, which for multiple reasons—including power outages, transportation delays, supplier disruptions, and more—affect their ability to deliver goods and services. Companies profiled in these pages have pioneered ways to better integrate previously disparate parts of the company to address a growing challenge, with manifold implications that require the combined effort of people with multiple talents and skills (e.g., Citi).

Resilience—a willingness and capacity to recover from calamity and creating alternative practices to adapt to new realities—is arguably an instinctive response to this multifaceted challenge that also boosts the human spirit and our natural sense of hope.

As we've seen in the foregoing chapters, some of the best news about extreme climate conditions like droughts and extreme events like storms, is that our changing climate can engender positive business response, preparation, and innovation. Indeed, we are witnessing many emerging business approaches—varying according to sector and company—to climate resilience.

To be sure, not all companies are as yet prepared and ready to adapt, as was reiterated at the Paris meetings and as the 2015 Adaptation Survey[1] makes clear (30 percent of companies surveyed say they don't have an adaptation plan in place). However, as recounted in preceding chapters, leading companies in strategic sectors are blazing new trails and taking steps that others can shape to fit their own needs and ends.

We've also seen that companies with a strong, long-standing sense of environmental and social purpose—with sustainability guidelines and

---

[1] Four Twenty-Seven Climate Solutions. (2015). Inside the Black Box: How Companies Prepare for Climate Change. Retrieved on February 29, 2016 from http://427mt.com/2015/05/inside-the-black-box-how-companies-prepare-for-climate-change/.

dedicated teams across silos—may more readily understand the new, riskier landscape, both physical and commercial, that climate change is already engendering. What's more, those companies, once aware of potential dangers ahead—awareness often gained through painful, first-hand experience of climate-related disaster—are more likely to both adapt (by developing resilience approaches) and mitigate. In the process, these companies are able to help abate climate change by finding ways to cut their GHG footprints and often those of their suppliers. The two strategies—adaptation and mitigation—rarely are mutually exclusive but instead often go hand in glove.

Finally, what climate change offers business is a challenge—in fact, an opportunity—to be met with business creativity, as we've seen throughout the foregoing chapters. Indeed, positive business change in the face of climate change—the subject of this closing chapter—is an inspiring response to what otherwise surely have been some of the most heartbreaking disasters of the past decade. Such business resilience is also a reminder that we do have the wisdom, talent, creativity, and urge to persist—not just commercially, but as hopeful and compassionate human beings—to help us tackle the ongoing challenges of climate change.

Perhaps unsurprisingly, some of these thoughts were voiced during the 2015 COP 21 in Paris—and subsequently, as companies begin to tackle the goals set there—where business was involved in the climate conversation as never before. Indeed, what those meetings demonstrated was a commitment on the part of business—companies, sectors, coalitions across industries, sometimes with guidance from NGOs—to put its cards on the table and commit to change by cutting emissions, moving to renewable energy, or combating climate change by other means. Hardly less important was Government actors' more solicitous—even welcoming—attitude toward the private sector and its involvement. Since the Accord was signed, companies have begun to tackle the goals it set out.

Indeed, as we've seen—notably in the chapter profiling some of IBM's efforts to improve and encourage communication and cooperation—ways to encourage business (along with broader public) climate resilience include: policies that may aid, incentivize, or even reward companies moving along this path; improved trust between public and private sectors to foster better ways of working jointly (sometimes dubbed public–private partnerships, or PPPs) toward solutions to a monumental problem affecting all; consumer and investor demands to prod companies to develop new products, services, markets, and ways of working; and progressive regulation (regionally, nationally, internationally) that incentivizes, or at least encourages, GHG reduction, and better communication and collaboration within companies and among them, as well as between businesses, NGOs, and governments.

Such ideas were broadly discussed in business forums at COP 21. Perhaps more important: some are also suggested in the Paris accord itself. Non-parties to the agreement, including companies, are invited to scale up efforts to reduce climate emissions, build resilience,[2] and share practices on mitigation and adaptation.[3] The Accord also acknowledges the role of "providing incentives for emissions reduction services, including tools such as domestic policies and carbon pricing."

In the run up to COP 21, business in the United States and beyond was already stepping up activity toward some of these goals, much of which was poised to accelerate in the wake of the Paris agreement and continues to move ahead.

In preparation for the Paris meeting, and reiterated there, companies in sectors from food and agriculture, banking, technology, real estate, and even Big Oil, put their cards on the table and committed to change— many even asking negotiators to "put a price on carbon." Sometimes this was done with others in the industry, sometimes in coalitions across industries, sometimes with guidance from NGOs or NGO coalitions (or even under the auspices of the White House).

During the year before COP 21, there were significant U.S. policy moves, on the federal and state levels, to urge business changes on climate, including the White House's Climate Action Plan to reduce emissions. Released in June 2015, the announcement that government contractors, such as IBM and United Technologies, would work to reduce GHGs suggested some fresh models for public–private partnerships. We

---

[2] United Nations Framework Convention on Climate Change (UNFCCC). *FCCC/CP/2015/L.9/Rev.1* Adoption of the Paris Agreement. Article 7, Paragraph 135.
[3] *FCCC/CP/2015/L.9/Rev.1.* Article 7, Paragraph 136.

watched the EPA announce new regulations on airlines to cut GHGs in June 2015, along with its later report on the economic risks of not cutting carbon.

In its March 2016 report, the Sustainability Responsibility Accounting Board (SASB), an independent nonprofit organization and an American National Standards Institute accredited standards developer, indicates that 154 US-based companies, representing more than $4.2 trillion in annual revenue, signed the American Business Act on Climate Pledge to show their support for climate action.[4]

Recently we've seen more universities take the symbolic move of divesting fossil fuel holdings in their investment portfolios. We've witnessed international governments taking daring new measures—such as France issuing new rules requiring institutional investors to disclose how they manage climate risk in June 2017, and Norway, one of the biggest oil-producing nations, divesting government pensions from coal investments in June 2015.[5] We saw European oil companies band together to ask the UN in May 2015 to help find ways to put a price on carbon to tackle climate change.

And who could ignore the heartening pledge of Microsoft's Bill Gates at the start of COP 21 to spend a billion dollars to launch the Breakthrough Energy Coalition, a group of private investors (28 billionaires from 10 countries partnered with 19 national governments) committed to early-stage investing in energy systems with near-zero carbon emissions (including a VIP list of investors, including Richard Branson of Virgin, Jeff Bezos of Amazon, and Mark Zuckerberg of Facebook)?[6]

---

[4]Sustainability Responsibility Accounting Board (SASB). Climate Risk SASB Technical Bulletin 2016-01. March 2016.

[5]Schwartz, J. (2015, January 6). Norway will Divest from Coal in Push Against Climate Change. *New York Times*. Retrieved February 29, 2016, from http://www.nytimes.com/2015/06/06/science/norway-in-push-against-climate-change-will-divest-from-coal.html.

[6]Wattles, J. (2015). "Bill Gates Launches Multi-billion Dollar Clean Energy Fund." *CNN Money.* November 13, 2015, accessed February 29, 2016. http://money.cnn.com/2015/11/29/news/economy/bill-gates-breakthrough-energy-coalition/.

Since the Paris agreement, such alliances have continued to make important strides. Not least: at the COP meetings themselves, government actors more inviting of the "private sector" than in the past, acknowledging the cooperation, or sometimes even leadership, of business, finance, and markets to achieve social goals like a low-carbon economy. By January 2016, nation-states were poised to deploy at least $16.5 trillion (estimated by the International Atomic Energy Association) to that end, as they make good on their Paris commitments.[7] This may encourage business to make greater commitments, as Ban-Ki Moon urged investors to do at a meeting at the UN in January 2016 in a follow-up to the Paris meetings.[8] The support and leadership of investors is crucial to addressing climate risks and capturing the opportunities this challenge presents. Many investors are already making progress.

But there is still a lot of work to be done. UN Secretary-General Ban Ki-moon challenged the investor community to "double—at a minimum—their clean energy investments by 2020." Among the most significant investment opportunities is the electric power sector, which—according to a new study released by Ceres and Bloomberg New Energy Finance—presents a $12 trillion opportunity for renewable power alone over the next 25 years.

Indeed, investors more generally are moving to lower carbon initiatives, whether voluntarily, as in the case including the ABP's pledge to quadruple its clean energy investment to €5 billion by 2020, or by decree, as in the case of French financial institutions, which are to report on carbon footprint of portfolio holdings from 2017.

---

[7]Wilkins, Michael. (2016). "The Paris Agreement: A New Dawn For Tackling Climate Change, Or More Of The Same?" *Standard and Poor's*. January 18, 2016, accessed February 29, 2016. https://www.globalcreditportal.com/ratingsdirect/renderArticle .do?articleId=1563652&SctArtId=364708&from=CM&nsl_code=LIME&sourceO bjectId=9482832&sourceRevId=1&fee_ind=N&exp_date=20260117-17:20:49.

[8]Fox, Christopher. (2016). "3 Ways the Paris Agreement will Expand Global Investment in Clean Energy." *Ceres*. January 8, 2016, accessed February 29, 2016 from https://www .ceres.org/issues/clean-trillion/realizing-the-clean-trillion-progress-and-challenges/3- ways-paris-climate-agreement-will-expand-global-investment-in-clean-energy.

From the launch of a new $2 billion low-carbon index fund as part of a $5 billion commitment to sustainable investments by New York State Comptroller Thomas P. DiNapoli, to the commitment from European pension fund ABP to reduce the carbon footprint of investment portfolios, investors and financial institutions are moving in the right direction on climate action.[9]

Finally, and perhaps most important, we've seen companies themselves looking for and finding opportunities to profit and serve alike, by embracing business innovation that stands to decrease the causes and devastating effects of climate change while helping people live healthier, safer, better lives.

We are not at the end of the resilience story but rather at another beginning point along a trajectory unfolding in real time. Post-Paris COP, business is likely to continue to adapt while mitigating climate change, particularly since the Accord itself highlights adaptation.[10] An important positive direction has been set, and companies are beginning to take next steps to embed climate goals into business aspirations and operations. In the case of the leaders profiled in this book, that likely will mean further adaptive measures. This forward movement on the part of business is likely to continue independently of any ongoing US Supreme Court stay of the Clean Power Plan, as stakeholders demand safer, healthier alternatives and companies look to cut energy costs.

This final chapter reviews some of the basic themes illustrated in foregoing chapters, which may suggest ways to help companies develop resilience approaches to the changing climate. Following the five themes that structure this book, priorities that companies can foster to develop resilience strategies include some relatively simple tools that can be adapted to multiple sectors and situations.

i. Responding to Weather

It's useful to consider how several of the companies in this book had direct encounters with extreme weather events: Citi's headquarters in downtown

---

[9] *FCCC/CP/2015/L.9/Rev.1.* Article 7, paragraph 25. Articles 9, 10 and 11.

[10] *FCCC/CP/2015/L.9/Rev.1.* Article 7, paragraph 25. Articles 9, 10 and 11.

Manhattan was directly affected by Hurricane Sandy, producing millions of dollars in damage; ConAgra's food supply was affected by drought in the western US. Other companies mentioned in these chapters have likewise been affected by these crises, including The Hartford and Sprint.

They have responded by changing some of what they do. For instance, Citi is raising some of its infrastructure so that it won't be flooded; likewise, the firm has created a low-energy data facility in London that it financed creatively. The firm is now offering that energy financing model to customers.

Others, mentioned in these chapters, have likewise applied hard knocks from extreme weather associated with climate change into their emerging business practices. They've been hurt, but they've been resilient: not only have they gotten back up off the mat, they've started to develop new ways of doing things—many of which will help their operations, their revenues, and the health of the planet. The Hartford, notably, has created a slew of insurance products to incentivize customers to use renewable energy.

ii. Learning from Disaster

While a number of companies profiled in these pages have been hurt by the extreme weather events of the last decade, they continue to learn from what they did—or didn't do—in those cases, and are mainstreaming adaptation mechanisms into their business practices.

A noteworthy case is Sprint, which, having experienced the Missouri floods, California wildfires, and Hurricanes Katrina and Sandy, reviews emergency preparedness measures on a frequent and regular basis, changing its practices in response to past events and in anticipation of a more uncertain future.

One of the prime examples of such continuous learning and institutionalization of adaptation measures into its larger sustainability framework is the company's backup energy system for emergencies. Communications, a vital service during crises, must be resilient. So the company continues to hone, update, and rework its systems in preparation for uncertainty ahead.

Incorporating learning into its business practices, the telecommunications company is also looking to offer its customers services to better warn in advance of potential events and to better communicate during and after them.

iii. Doing More with Less

As climate change draws our attention to natural resources—e.g., water scarcity—some companies, notably in the agricultural and food industry, are already preparing and changing in response. Importantly, that entails finding innovative ways to make the supply and value chains more efficient—and less costly—by modifying growing techniques, improving production, simplifying transportation and slashing waste.

ConAgra is partnering extensively with its farmer suppliers to help them use advanced watering techniques in the drought-ridden western U.S., where the company sources its tomatoes. It has also changed where it produces tomato sauce—which used to be shipped from Tennessee all the way to Canada—thereby slashing transportation and energy costs as well as cutting its GHG emissions. The company has also discovered ways to retrieve what was once considered food waste carted to landfill from its facilities by turning it into viable food products it now sells, sometimes to new markets, like prisons.

Likewise, Stonyfield Farm, anticipating ongoing disruptions to organic milk sources, partly related to climate change, has launched a new training program for organic dairy farmers who can produce organic milk to sell to the company. What's more, the training farm, along with the farms to be run by the trainees, are to be near enough to Stonyfield's headquarters that the company can cut transport distance, and therefore GHG emissions, of hauls.

iv. Taking a Risk—and Managing it

All the companies profiled in these chapters are taking risks in response to the larger climate risks they face. Citi is developing new products for new markets, as is ConAgra. Yet, these additional risks must also be managed.

Traditionally, companies have managed risk by buying insurance, and insurers are steeped in risks of all sorts—from operational to financial. Climate risk affects all risks for business, individuals, as well as the insurers themselves. As a risk-centered business, insurance (perhaps unsurprisingly) has been among the first to embrace enterprise risk management. The Hartford, a two century-old company, exemplifies leadership in climate resilience as it takes on new risks (introducing new products and insuring new markets) and manages them—for instance, backing up data off-site to ensure business continuity, while advising its customers to do so, too. At the same time, it has incentivized employees to reduce GHGs by giving them opportunities to work from home and to charge electric vehicles at company headquarters.

As a risk-centered business, The Hartford also has demonstrated its own resilience in seeking the upside of the risks—opportunities to insure new industries, to create new products, and to respond to new markets. It has also developed an internal climate resilience approach that embraces some of the same above-mentioned changes, including business continuity elements, such as off-site data backup.

v. Communicating Change, Collaborating on Climate

One reason it's difficult to decide how to adapt in the face of climate change and how to build a resilience strategy is the uncertainty climate change entails, which, in turn, makes it harder to communicate.

As has been illustrated in the case of companies profiled here, an effective resilience strategy requires cooperation and collaboration, mainly because no one person has all the information or answers to a complicated problem. Effective collaboration requires communication, something that's often taken for granted inside companies and among business, government, and civil society.

Working with Suffolk County in New York, IBM offered a three-step approach to communicating climate risk that can be modified to suit multiple situations, in communities and companies alike: understand the problem and boost awareness; examine the data that exist and simplify through various means, including deleting, synchronizing, and updating; and engaging the community through ordinary means, including live meetings, education, and social media.

Making—and Avoiding—Mistakes

Finally, a whole chapter could be devoted to making—and avoiding—mistakes. None of the companies in this book has ventured forward without having erred. Mistakes are inherent to change. Yet, as we've seen, from Sprint to ConAgra to Citi, it is critical to acknowledge the past, learn from errors, and prepare to avoid them in the face of more change ahead. This is a process for all—from communities to cities to countries and companies alike. One advantage for business is its appetite for opportunity, from which creative solutions to ever-new needs and problems are likely to arise. A mistake can prepare a company to take on new challenges, not least the increased threats to facilities, employees, communities, and operations almost inevitably posed by greater frequency and intensity of weather events.

In response to the past and looking forward, companies are more likely to develop ways, or even methodologies to ascertain and plan for potential risks—including not just how to protect against them, but how potentially to profit in a variety of ways, from improved reputation to higher bottom-line results.

Mistakes are virtually inevitable, even for the best of companies. What's critical is that the experience not be forgotten or wasted. Mistakes offer the opportunity to correct what's not working, improve, and create something better.

Opportunity and Innovation

Most important is the lesson that to address climate risk, there may be nothing that business is better at than seeking and seizing opportunities generally arising from pressing needs while forging innovative solutions. Business has long adapted to new circumstances and challenges, and business is good at taking the necessary risks to address new problems. The private sector can often act more nimbly than the public. That's why it's critical that as companies consider guidelines, they also use their creativity to mold them independently to their own goals.

Index

THE GIVING VOICE TO VALUES ON BUSINESS ETHICS AND CORPORATE SOCIAL RESPONSIBILITY COLLECTION

Mary Gentile, *Editor*

The Giving Voice To Values initiative teamed up with Business Expert Press to produce a collection of books on Business Ethics and Corporate Social Responsibility that will bring a practical, solutions-oriented, skill-building approach to the salient questions of values-driven leadership. Giving Voice To Values (www.GivingVoiceToValues.org)—the curriculum, the pedagogy and the research upon which it is based—was designed to transform the foundational assumptions upon which the teaching of business ethics is based, and importantly, to equip future business leaders to not only know what is right, but how to make it happen.

Other Titles in This Collection

- *Ethical Leadership in Sport: What's Your ENDgame?* by Pippa Grange
- *The ART of Responsible Communication: Leading With Values Every Day* by David L. Remund
- *Engaging Millennials for Ethical Leadership: What Works For Young Professionals and Their Managers* by Jessica McManus Warnell
- *Sales Ethics: How To Sell Effectively While Doing the Right Thing* by Alberto Aleo and Alice Alessandri
- *Working Ethically in Finance: Clarifying Our Vocation* by Anthony Asher
- *A Strategic and Tactical Approach to Global Business Ethics, Second Edition* by Lawrence A. Beer
- *Shaping the Future of Work: What Future Worker, Business, Government, and Education Leaders Need To Do For All To Prosper* by Thomas A. Kochan
- *War Stories: Fighting, Competing, Imagining, Leading* by Leigh Hafrey

Announcing the Business Expert Press Digital Library

Concise e-books business students need for classroom and research

This book can also be purchased in an e-book collection by your library as

- *a one-time purchase,*
- *that is owned forever,*
- *allows for simultaneous readers,*
- *has no restrictions on printing, and*
- *can be downloaded as PDFs from within the library community.*

Our digital library collections are a great solution to beat the rising cost of textbooks. E-books can be loaded into their course management systems or onto students' e-book readers.
The **Business Expert Press** digital libraries are very affordable, with no obligation to buy in future years. For more information, please visit **www.businessexpertpress.com/librarians**. To set up a trial in the United States, please email **sales@businessexpertpress.com**

CPSIA information can be obtained
at www.ICGtesting.com
Printed in the USA
JSHW032316261122
33723JS00003B/126